Ira Rakatan

Edited by John Caserta and Lynnette Widder

Ira Rakatansky
As Modern
As Tomorrow

Essays by Joan Ockman and Lynnette Widder
Photographs by Thad Russell and John Caserta

Rhode Island School of Design Architecture Series
William Stout Publishers

William Stout Publishers
1326 – 1328 South 51st Street
Richmond, CA 94804 USA
stoutpublishers.com

Rhode Island School of Design
Department of Architecture
Bayard Ewing Building
231 South Main Street
Providence, RI 02903 USA
architecture.risd.edu

Other books in the RISD Architecture Series
may be found at architecture.risd.edu/ras

ISBN: 978-0-9819667-0-0
Library of Congress Control Number: 2009941913

Printed in China

Photographs on previous two spreads are of
Ira Rakatansky, Lenore Gray and their daughter
Lynn at their first home in Lincoln, Rhode Island

Contents

r area of 36 by 40 feet lent itself to few rooms, none of tremendous pro-

winter comes and the flowers go, young trees and shrubs will carry on in the well-organized pattern.

f the conversion from stable to contemporary dwelling are discussed by Mrs. Miller and an

Introduction

The architecture produced by Ira Rakatansky during his prolific career in Rhode Island, which began some sixty-five years ago, well deserves a broader audience. The work is readily appreciated for its well-proportioned spaces, realized in simple but stunning material palettes, set in strong relation to light and landscape. It can also be understood within the context of post-war American modernism, as evidence of the symbiosis between lifestyle and architectural creativity. It bears witness to the ways in which Rakatansky invested his own convictions in the architecture he effected. The images, drawings, descriptive texts and essays in this book are calculated to support all these readings.

Returning to Providence in 1946 after attending Harvard for three years to earn a Master's degree, Rakatansky was faced with some advantages, and some considerable disadvantages, in his mission to realize architecture to the high standards set by his international and highly intellectual group of professors and students. His familial relationships, his contact

with local craftspeople and his ability to create a web of personal and professional connections were well-served by Providence, where a stream of mostly self-made, first or second generation Americans had begun to commission architecture.

On the other hand, the city's dominant architectural fabric was its Colonial-era wood houses and its 19th-century industrial buildings. As a modern architect, especially with his educational pedigree, Rakatansky was alone. He was not part of a like-minded architectural community, except through the journals to which he subscribed or the correspondence he kept; rather, the way he made architecture was an individual vocation.

And although he trained a succession of excellent architects in his office, there is no 'school of Rakatansky'.

The spaces in Rakatansky's realized projects express the pleasure, not the struggle, of being an architect under these conditions. The idea that architecture is 'an enclosure of space around life for the specific site' remains his core architectural belief; his enormous empathy with his clients is apparent in the emotional investment which allows him even decades later to recall specific details about the family members, children's hobbies and domestic habits of clients whose great grandchildren might now be living in the houses he built for them. The pleasure he found in his work, and that his clients found in inhabiting it, is also evident in the spaces, small in dimension but expansive in the qualities of light and diversity of relationships between interior and exterior.

This same pleasure suffuses the moments when he allowed himself some slight idiosyncrasy—an enormous eleven-foot-high front door to a compact home, a swath of blue tile creeping across the kitchen threshold and onto the wooden living room floor, slipped alignments among a house's windows which take a façade from the banal register of merely expressing interior space to the realm of compositional dexterity.

We began looking at Rakatansky's architecture more than five years ago.

Based upon our different trainings – as an architect, or as a designer and photographer – we looked differently. Documented in contemporary photos and in carefully retrieved archival material is the way in which personal objects, some exuding desuetude and others testing the spaces' robustness by means of their unconcerned inappropriateness, occupy spaces conceived some fifty years ago. Given equal weight are the drawings that map those spaces orthographically, and communicate how they were realized. Each building rediscovered, each archived article found, each personal story related, has provided new insights. Rakatansky's work is consistent without being repetitive.

second story noses
e long flat main roof.
flat roof of the upper

a passageway extending from the
living room to the bedroom area.

At the beginning of the pas-

grows a flue encased in a huge
white concrete tube. A matching stack rising from the floor
at the right end of the fire-

dar decking
ly polished
ing room
stairs bed

has white cabinetwork and light-brown floor covering counter tops. In lower part of open-e
ments for electrical appliances and trays. Shelves pull out of low corner cupboard where Mrs.

It evidences his persuasive-
ness, but also his creative
flexibility and his capacity to
reflect upon specific localized
demands without compro-
mising the coherence of his
work within the philosophical
parameters of Modernism.
There is much to gain from
looking at his works. They
are fine examples of architectural skill; they are articulate
documents of evolving ways
of life, negotiated in space;
they represent a wealth of
construction knowledge;
and they are evidence of that
to which we aspire — that
architecture and design are
expressions of the pleasure
in creative dialogue.

— THE EDITORS

Why Is a Modern House
Joan Ockman

When and how did the American house become modern? Historians
of twentieth-century architecture have given differing explanations.
According to one, the modern movement originated in Europe and
was imported to the United States in the 1930s by leading émigré
architects like Walter Gropius, Marcel Breuer, Ludwig Mies van der
Rohe, and Laszlo Moholy-Nagy. These refugees from totalitarianism
took up posts at major American design schools where they dissem-
inated their new vision of architecture. According to another, the
'shift to modern' was largely catalyzed by World War II, when mecha-
nized production took command of the national imagination and a
newly receptive climate for rational planning and functional aesthet-
ics emerged. Yet a third explanation has it that the most advanced
building in the United States was already modern in technology and
construction, if not in style, well before the 1930s. This indigenous
evolution was derailed by the Depression but was to resurface later.
Frank Lloyd Wright's domestic architecture from the 1890s onward
constituted an original American development, bearing out Gertrude
Stein's statement that the United States should be considered 'the
oldest country in the world' since it was first to embrace twentieth-
century civilization.[1]

Mrs. Bruno Franek, 1955

These three narratives, actually more convergent than competing, offer a useful framework within which to situate the exemplary career of Ira Rakatansky, the architect whose prolific but not widely known body of residential work is the focus of this book. The son of a builder in Providence, Rhode Island, Rakatansky was educated under Gropius and Breuer at Harvard and opened his practice just after World War II.

THE EDUCATION OF A MODERN AMERICAN ARCHITECT

Ira Rakatansky entered Harvard's architecture school in 1943 after obtaining a four-year certificate of graduation from Rhode Island School of Design.[2] He received his B.Arch. from Harvard in 1945, then remained one more year to obtain his Master's as a Wheelwright Fellow. Having been exempted from military service because of his weak eyesight, and searching for a professional program within proximity of Providence, Rakatansky found Harvard more accessible at this date than MIT, which required greater preparation in the sciences. The military deployment had also depleted Harvard's enrollment, and to fill out its student body during the war years the architecture school began admitting women for the first time as well as students who did not already hold a B.A. It also open-ed its doors to a greater number of applicants who came from outside its traditional demography. Rakatansky, who was Jewish, thus found himself in surprisingly diverse company, his classmates including, besides women, many foreign students, at least one African-American (who, after Rakatansky received the Wheelwright Fellowship, took over a teaching assignment for him), and others who might not have gained admission under different circumstances. Among the classmates and colleagues with whom he became friendly at

Harvard were Harry Seidler from Australia, I. M. Pei, Peter Oberlander and Cornelia Hahn (later Oberlander), and Anne Tyng. Philip Johnson had graduated in 1943 but was still around Cambridge when Rakatansky arrived, living in the modernist house he had built for himself as a Master's thesis project. He also met William Wurster, an older student in the urban planning program who left in 1944 to take up the deanship of the architecture school at MIT, and Wurster's wife, the housing expert Catherine Bauer, who would teach a socially oriented housing seminar at the GSD for several years starting in 1946. Rakatansky did not enter much into the life of the larger university, by his own account, perhaps feeling somewhat out of his depth intellectually; on weekends he often took the train home to Providence.[3]

But it was his encounter with the former Bauhaus masters Gropius and Breuer that provided a decisive formation for the young student. Harvard had been put on a modern course in 1936 by Joseph Hudnut, when he became dean of the renamed Graduate School of Design and succeeded in hiring Gropius, the founding director of the world-famous Bauhaus in Weimar Germany, as chair of the architecture department. With Gropius's arrival the following year the school acquired avant-garde luster and was propelled in its new direction. Gropius not only quickly surrounded himself with former colleagues from Germany, including Breuer and Martin Wagner, but he also set out to institute a course in design fundamentals along the lines of the pioneering *Vorkurs* at the Bauhaus. The aim was to inculcate in first-year students a universal visual language geared to the demands of a modern industrial society; emphasis was on analysis of the psychological and physiological effects of basic shapes, material properties, and spatial relationships, as well as their functional

Top: Walter Gropius with students; Rakatansky third from right
Top Right: Rakatansky at Harvard, circa 1944
Bottom: Rakatansky presenting bachelor's thesis

implications. Unexpectedly, the course ran into major resistance from Hudnut, who by the mid-1940s was becoming increasingly disenchanted with the ahistorical and professionalized formalism of Gropius's approach. The latter was antithetical philosophically to his own interest in urban, civic values and in a more humanistic attitude toward dwelling. Hudnut further objected to the schism between the creative and practical sides of architecture implicit in Gropius's conception of design fundamentals, a holdover from the division of the curriculum at the Bauhaus into form-making workshops and craft or building workshops. Hudnut thus effectively blocked Gropius's repeated attempts to have Josef Albers, another émigré Bauhaus master then teaching at Black Mountain College in North Carolina, hired to teach the course. In 1952 the internal 'struggle for modernism' between Gropius and Hudnut ended with design fundamentals being dropped from the GSD curriculum and Gropius's highly public resignation from the architecture department.[4]

In the mid-forties, however, the acrimony brewing between the two Harvard educators apparently entered the consciousness of most of its architecture students only peripherally. Rakatansky did not have much direct involvement with Hudnut, although he speaks of him today with admiration. His most important mentors were Gropius and Breuer, as mentioned, and Hugh Stubbins, a former student hired as an assistant professor in 1941 to replace Breuer as Gropius's assistant. Rakatansky recalls 'Pius' (Gropius's nickname) presiding over critiques in Robinson Hall with elegant and aloof formality, emanating the aura of the great man. But he and his wife Ise also graciously welcomed students on visits to their house in suburban Lincoln, a showcase of modernist precepts that Gropius realized in 1937–38 in collaboration with

Breuer; and on occasion he also paused at students' drafting tables to offer hands-on advice concerning practical matters of construction and technique.[5] Lajko (Breuer's nickname), on the other hand, was genial and warm and not above going out with his students for a drink. Rakatansky recalls him with great affection. In 1945 Breuer hired Rakatansky to help him in his office on working drawings for the Geller House. This was the first of Breuer's seminal 'binuclear' schemes: the living-dining-kitchen space was separated from the bedrooms by a central entry foyer, and the two wings of the composition were topped by a butterfly roof. Rakatansky would employ a similar plan arrangement and roof form in his Weisberg and Falk houses, completed in 1949 and 1954.

Yet it may not be a great exaggeration to say that the German architects were affected by their encounter with American education and building culture almost as much as the latter were transformed by them. The large, powerful university in mid-20th-century America was obviously an entirely different kind of institution from the avant-garde design school struggling for survival amid the Weimar Republic's growing political hostility and cultural conservatism, forced to decamp from Weimar to Dessau to Berlin before the Nazis finally caused it to close its doors. Harvard's affluence and academic authority gave the 'Bauhaus idea' a decidedly different complexion once it was transplanted; the concept of 'totality' Gropius had espoused earlier in his career as a vision of the scope of modern design gave way to 'teamwork' in the more corporative environment of the mid-20th-century Cambridge research university. With respect to the subject of housing and its teaching, Gropius remained throughout his career a champion of the low-cost, high-rise residential block or slab, on the model of his early *Siedlungen*. Yet at

Harvard he also addressed himself earnestly to the problem of the 'postwar dwelling for the average family'. In the briefs he gave to students from 1943 (or earlier) through the early 1950s, the program was defined as a single-family detached house with a garage or carport located in a landscaped suburban neighborhood. This intrinsically American assignment laid special emphasis on 'visual variety' as a means of counteracting the negative effects of regimentation and impersonality endemic to a standardized system of planning and construction.[6]

Gropius and Breuer's view of architecture was altered not only by the new social and economic circumstances they had to confront in mid-century America, however, but also by American building practice. This is not surprising given the strong interest of both in methods and issues of construction. The impact of the New England vernacular and in particular of wood structures — wood being the cheapest and most available building material during the Depression and war years — is manifest in the houses they built for themselves in Lincoln, Massachusetts, shortly after they arrived, which combined native fieldstone, brick, and wood with industrial materials like glass block, chrome, and acoustical plaster. They also carefully studied the American balloon frame construction with their students. Invented in the nineteenth century to permit rapid construction using standard-dimension lumber and light nailing, the balloon frame contrasted with the heavier timber post-and-beam carpentry typical in Europe. As architectural historian William Jordy has written, "The American structural tradition favored the frame rather than the wall and depended on a high degree of prefabrication of building parts that could be assembled rapidly and easily by a labor force that, by European standards, was at once scarce and

Rakatansky worked for Marcel Breuer during his first year at Harvard. One of the projects he drafted was the Geller House on Long Island.

expensive, in part specialized and in part ill-trained."[7] Gropius also incorporated this knowledge into a wood prefabrication 'kit' called the Packaged House System that he developed in the 1940s in partnership with another émigré compatriot, Konrad Wachsmann. The Packaged House picked up on schemes for industrialized housing, and specifically jointed panels, with which both architects had experimented in the 1920s and 1930s in Germany. But while in the earlier work Gropius had minimized the separateness of the units, in the American work he "intensified the sense of their discreteness to make visible their coming together." Thus, "the emphasis on the container in Europe [became] an emphasis on the component in America."[8]

"Germans are systematic," Breuer generalized; "Americans are efficient."[9] The accommodation by Gropius and Breuer of European theory to American facts undoubtedly found an especially receptive student at the GSD in Rakatansky. Rakatansky had entered Harvard with firsthand knowledge of standard American building practice, acquired through summers spent working on the construction sites of his father, a speculative building contractor. This not only gave him sufficient practical experience to be excused from Hugh Stubbins' first-year course in construction, required of all incoming architecture students at Harvard, but also prepared him well to assimilate and adapt his teachers' radical ideas.

THE POSTWAR HOUSE

While Harvard was imparting its Bauhaus-derived pedagogy to the profession's future elite, the Depression and especially the war years were fostering a wider popular acceptance of modern architecture. Up to the 1930s, American taste had remained deeply conservative, especially in the domestic realm. With the onset of the economic crisis, however, new winds began to blow. "It was disgrace and hardship that gave the style known as Modern its chance," as Russell Lynes wrote in *The Tastemakers*. If the basic settlements built by reform-minded government planners on the outskirts of cities to cope with a desperate housing situation were "singularly lacking in the promise of joy"— clusters of single-story, flat-roofed boxes of minimal dimension — they were also "happier than the slums."[10] At the same time, another, more escapist version of modern was finding its way into American culture, from streamlined department-store furnishings, Hollywood movie interiors, and gasoline stations to the 1939 New York World's Fair. Hybridizing traditionalist and modernist impulses, the new style was often disparagingly labeled 'modernistic'.

But with the conversion of the economy to military production, another mentality emerged. Wartime research and development not only spurred new construction technologies, encouraging the growth of industries like prefabrication and electronics, and making use of materials like plywood, metal alloys, plastics, and synthetic resins, with direct future applicability to the domestic market. It also implanted a new attitude toward functional design. "After many decades of functionalist preaching, this century is today producing functionally designed objects for the first time on a tremendous scale," declared the editors of *Architectural Forum* in 1943. "In other words, in an extreme emergency we turn unquestioning to functional design. It is important to note that these products of ingenuity, economy, and utmost exploitation of limited materials have quite unconsciously become the most satisfying designs of our machine civilization."[11]

At the same time, especially once the Allied victory was in reach by mid-1943, government planners, advertisers of consumer goods, and others — including out-of-work architects — began turning their sights to the period ahead. Concerned with how to sustain the American economy at peak productivity when the mobilization ended so that the country would not slide back into another depression, and eager to whet the appetite of citizens who had suffered privations not just on the battlefront but also at home, planners in Washington spoke of "mobilizing for abundance" while pundits painted giddy pictures of a "thermoplastic, aerodynamic, supersonic, electronic, gadgetonic" postwar world.[12] The architecture magazines, for their part, published optimistic predictions about the boom in housing that would occur once the GI's began returning home. "The existing backlog of needs and desires for better living quarters is greater than anything in history," stated the editors of *Pencil Points* in an introduction to a feature titled "Houses for the People" that appeared in September 1945. "All prophets seem to be agreed that [after the war] there will be built in the United States from 800,000 to 1,250,000 dwelling units a year for the next ten years. In the face of such a tremendous prospect, many persons and organizations heretofore only casually interested in residential building are feverishly awaiting the production and release of materials and equipment so that they may ride profitably on the bandwagon." Noting that the six-room house for $6,000 was "the most popular goal," the editors of the magazine — soon to be renamed *Progressive Architecture* in a symbolic shift — went on to observe "a distinct and strong trend away from traditional types of design and toward what has come rather vaguely to be called 'modern'."[13]

The wartime atmosphere of patriotic solidarity, altruism, and egalitarianism also had more social and ideological effects. It deepened the desire to popularize and extend the progressivist aspirations of modern architecture to average American citizens. As the historian of American advertising Roland Marchand has written, "The explicitly democratic themes of wartime popular culture promoted unity. Morale-builders stressed the idea of equal sacrifices…. The war years also prolonged the modest redistribution of income from rich to poor that had begun during the 1930s. Although this process was to come to a standstill in the late 1940s, Americans emerged from the war confident of a snowballing trend toward economic democratization and a classless culture."[14] The mixture of anticipatory consumerism with wartime civicism was exemplified by an advertising campaign that was launched by the Revere Copper and Brass Company in 1941 and ran through 1944. A leading manufacturer of pots and pans, Revere was forced to curtail its domestic production during the war by the rationing of metals, but like other producers of household goods and services it continued to advertise widely as a way of keeping its wares in the public eye. Running from 1941 to 1944 in both architecture magazines and mass-market publications like *The Saturday Evening Post* under the title "Revere's Part in Better Living," the campaign promoted innovative schemes for the postwar house solicited from a significant group of modernist designers and architects. The majority of them, which were also published separately as illustrated pamphlets, were for inexpensive single-family houses and featured flexible and expandable layouts, time-saving kitchens tailored to the postwar servantless household, and ample built-in storage space. Although a number of the schemes were based on prefabricated components and standardized assembly, a statement by the company president stressed strongly that "Americans want 'living', not housing." [15]

The proselytizing of flexible and unfettered modern living space and of an individualistic as opposed to collective and anonymous mode of dwelling was also carried out in countless other American publications of the 1940s, and it was directed to everyone from the professional architect to the consumer, and most particularly the housewife. 'Mrs. Consumer' would become a driving force of the postwar American economy. Among the more carefully presented arguments on be-half of modern architecture as a fresh and direct approach to living, "an attitude towards life" rather than an imitative style, was an exhibition catalogue of 1946 published by the Museum of Modern Art. Put together by curator Elizabeth Mock, who had been a member of Frank Lloyd Wright's Taliesin Fellowship in the early 1930s (and was also the younger sister of Catherine Bauer), *If You Want to Build a House* was a kind of primer for postwar American families. [16] Another publication in the same vein was George Nelson and Henry Wright's *Tomorrow's House* (1945), subtitled *How to Plan Your Post-War Home Now*, in which the authors — well-known architects and designers, and editors of the journal *Architectural Forum* — laid out their "theory of storage." [17] The latter basically amounted to designing expanded partition walls and built-in units to contain the owners' myriad possessions. Yet the unstated subtext of this paradigmatic exemplar of American modernist ideology at a nascent moment of American consumer culture may be said to be a sort of ethic of inconspicuous accumulation, a morality of consumption.

Among other mid-century evangelists of the modern American house were James and Katherine Morrow Ford, a husband-wife team whose own house was among those designed by Breuer and Gropius in Lincoln in the late 1930s, and who were responsible for several well-researched and illustrated books on the subject. In the opening paragraph of their successful *The Modern House in America* (initially published in 1940 and reprinted several times throughout the decade), the Fords posed and answered the question "What is modern?" by stating: "The essence of the new residential architecture is revealed in its twofold purpose: to base its plans upon the organic life of the family to be housed, and to make logical use of the products of invention. It has elected to make a fresh approach, to free itself of constraints, by consciously ignoring tradition and the expectations which the latter imposes with regard to façade and plan. The outer form of the modern house becomes the outgrowth of a plan built around the interests, routine activities, and aspirations of the client and his family...." [18] In other words, the modern American house was not to be based on an abstract social idea, like its counterparts in Europe, nor was it to be rigid and doctrinaire in form. Its "essence" had to do with satisfying the "organic" needs of the American family and incorporating contemporary technology.

This was the context of practical idealism in which Ira Rakatansky undertook to build his first houses after the war. In the tradition of many young architects, one of his initial commissions was for a relative, his sister. Realized in 1947 with the collaboration of his father, the Sumner Halsband house in East Greenwich, Rhode Island, was a modest rectangular volume sheathed in scored plywood, with five rooms, no basement, and a flat roof whose three-foot overhang dipped slightly on the south and west to shield those elevations from direct sunlight. In April 1949 it appeared in a feature article titled "WHY Is a Modern House?" published in a women's housekeeping magazine called *Splendor*. In the view of the author — and echoing the litany of American shelter literature almost verbatim — Rakatansky's house precisely answered the needs of the postwar family:

"The modern house is because civilization has changed. It is because homes have few if any servants. It is because the modern family is small. It is because … each room must serve several purposes. It is because more young people of modest means are building homes today.

"The modern house is because architects are taking a new approach to building. Traditional houses were built from the outside in….

"The modern house has no ornamentation. Its parts are plain, simple and functional.

"The modern house is because woman's place is no longer in the home for 24 hours a day. The modern woman wants a house that can be easily cleaned and kept neat, that has plenty of easily accessible storage space, that is compact enough to watch the baby, do her washing and prepare dinner at the same time…."[19]

A NEW VERNACULAR?

In fact, the shift to modern after World War II would be neither so widespread nor so transformative as its most fervent proponents hoped. With the return to normalcy soon unsettled by new insecurities, both political and psychological, in the new atmosphere of the Cold War, the idea of the American house was inflected not just by practical realities but also by the desire for a more rooted and reassuring image of domesticity. The wartime dream of the prefabricated dwelling cheaply mass-produced on the model of the car or airplane — from Buckminster Fuller's Dymaxion to Gropius and Wachsmann's Packaged House System to ill-fated startups to come like Carl Koch's Acorn and Lustron schemes — had seemed to have a real moment of possibility in the war's immediate aftermath, when the correctly predicted housing shortage made people willing to accept unconventional solutions, "to live in anything, even Quonset huts."[20] Yet as a population sick of wartime makeshift, impermanence, and regimentation, and primed for coming affluence, began to pursue its pent-up nesting instincts, the luster of the factory-built dwelling machine faded along with wilder visions of cloud cars and revolving houses. By the end of the 1940s a developer like William Levitt, among others, knew how to capitalize on the new national mood. With astute entrepreneurial instincts, he effectively cloaked a highly standardized and Taylorized construction process — based on his wartime experience building military barracks and emergency housing — in the familiar guise of a bungalow, and stocked it with a washing machine and a television set (the latter a brand-new commodity at this date). Not surprisingly, American home buyers flocked in massive numbers to his Levittown tract houses on Long Island and in suburban Philadelphia, where acres of farmland were being transformed overnight.

At a high-culture level, a contentious symposium took place at the Museum of Modern Art in early 1948. Titled "What Is Happening to Modern Architecture?" it was a kind of summit meeting convened in response to an article published a couple months earlier by the critic Lewis Mumford in his Skyline column in the *New Yorker*. Besides Mumford, the main speakers included Alfred Barr, Jr., and Henry-Russell Hitchcock, Gropius and Breuer, George Nelson and Peter Blake (among others). In his column Mumford had denounced the "so-called international style of the nineteen-thirties," explicitly attacking the famous exhibition that Hitchcock and Philip

Johnson had curated at the Museum in 1932.[21] This exhibition, which had preceded the main wave of emigration by the European architects by a few years, had not only helped to prepare the ground for the their arrival. It had also served to repackage the European movement for American consumption by placing primary emphasis on the stylistic features of the new architecture and there-by downplaying the movement's political and social background. The focus on expensive villas by the masters rather than collective housing projects made their radical work — as Mumford's protégée Catherine Bauer put it at the time — "safe for millionaires."[22] Fifteen years later Mumford argued that the "glorification of the mechanical and the impersonal and the aesthetically puritanic" by the academic American imitators of Le Corbusier, Mies van der Rohe, and Gropius had become passé, superseded by a more "native and humane form of modernism." He associated this new regionally inflected sensibility especially with the work of William Wurster — who would shortly leave MIT to return to his practice in the San Francisco area — and with Wurster's predecessors Bernard Maybeck and Gardner Dailey, calling their domestic architecture "a free yet unobtrusive expression of the terrain, the climate, and the way of life on the Coast." While Mumford took the Bay Region as his primary example in the article, he also noted that "[s]ome of the best examples of this at once native and universal tradition are being built in New England."[23]

Predictably enough, Mumford's provocation elicited a strong response from those invited to the symposium at MoMA. In his intervention, Gropius accused the critic of chauvinistic sentimentality, on the one hand arguing that European modernism had never truly been antagonistic to its surroundings, and on the other asking, "Do we want to have Chicken à la King with Ferro-Concrete Sauce

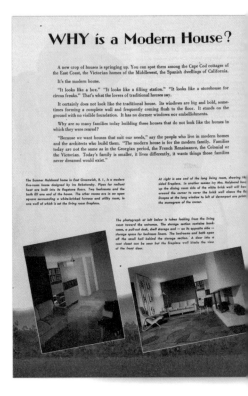

Popular magazines were early advocates of Rakatansky's work. The publications introduced readers to modern residential architecture with an optimistic use of photos, headline typography and descriptive text. At top is *Splendor* Magazine from April 1949; to its right, *BOXOFFICE* Magazine from October 1957; at right, *Perfect Home* from July 1950; at far right *The Providence Journal* from October 1948. This feature on the Halsband House was the first of many *Journal* articles written by Dorothy Agnew, who followed Rakatansky's work until the late 1950s. This book reprints many of her articles.

A 'SUNKEN' PLAYGROUND FOR SAFETY

Fencing and Supervision Also Contribute to Safety at New $500,000 Drive-In

The new 1,650-car Shipyard Drive-In Theatre, Providence, R. I., which takes its name from nearby shipyards, has many unusual features, including this sunken playground. It is located in front of this terrace patio, adjacent to the concessions building. Divided into two sections, the playground offers the Tot Lot at right, the regular children's playground in the center, and a miniature golf course at left. The Shipyard is located in the center of town.

WITH THE vigorous enthusiasm of a still-young industry, drive-in theatre exhibition keeps coming up with innovations in design and operation. Typical, is the new one-half-million dollar, 1,650-car Shipyard Drive-In Theatre in Providence, R. I., with many special features, including a sunken playground, an extraordinary concessions building, two dance patios, a terrace patio and three suspended boxoffices serving six lanes of traffic.

The playground was sunk in front of the terrace patio adjacent to the concessions building for three reasons: first and principally, for greater safety for children; sec-

ond, so that the area could be used while the picture is on the screen, as it is downlit; third, for more eye appeal.

The playground is divided into three sections. On the extreme right is the Tot Lot, with sandboxes, small slides and swings, which older children are not permitted to enter. In the center is the regular playground for older children with a merry-go-round, slides and swings, ferris wheel, larger slides and swings and a miniature train. The miniature train sports a 750-foot track around the entire playland and goes through a tunnel, the top of which serves as the patio terrace with 60 chairs. The

tunnel serves also as a storage place for the train at night.

An attendant is on duty at all times the playgrounds are open.

The third section of the playground is the miniature golf course for adults. Only children with adults can enter this section. The free golf course of nine holes was designed by Philip Lowe, associated with the Rifkin circuit in this venture. It has landscaped flowers and water holes, but Lowe frankly admits that he wanted something to "put people at ease," something to allow as many as want to, to play it. For those who do not want to play, the kiddies are in view and they can enjoy the terrace patio as well.

PORTABLE [...]

There are three concessions stands in the playground where the attendant will sell candy floss and [...]

The ground [...] paved in soft [...] ber matting. [...] Tot Lot is fe [...] dren's lot, an [...] is surrounded [...] from sight to [...] above ground [...] ated between [...] the concessions [...] size.

The entire [...] surrounded [...] steel fencing [...]

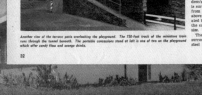

Another view of the terrace patio overlooking the playground. The 750-foot track of the miniature train runs through the tunnel beneath. The portable concessions stand at left is one of two on the playground which offer candy floss and orange drinks.

32

colored panels. These are attractively illuminated in the following unique manner: every 18 feet of the fencing are lights, white lights on the outside of the theatre, blue lights on the inside. These lights are fluorescent and cast a soft blue haze around the rear of the theatre as cars are leaving.

The three boxoffices are most unusual in that they are suspended from a steel overhead canopy of modern design. The boxoffices are made of concrete-treated acoustical board and are painted in three pastels, each booth a different color. They are downlit. Large teardrop plantings flank the six entrance lanes.

TWO DANCE PATIOS

On either side of the concessions building, located between ramps eight and 13, are dance patios. The theatre has a direct line to Station WICE, Providence, where a disc jockey spins records from the theatre, starting at 7 p.m. The broadcasting system is installed directly into the sound system of the theatre, so that the disc jockey needs to bring no equipment with him. He spins records for dancing at the theatre three nights a week, and twice each week free dance instruction is given to early bird theatre patrons.

Each individual speaker to the cars is a one-watt system. There are twin tower moonlight poles for lighting.

The refreshment facilities at the Shipyard are the result of industry-wide cooperation in design and planning. Philip and Samuel Lowe Jr., who have operated Theatre Candy Co., Inc., in Boston for the past 20 years, drew on their experience in designing and equipping refreshment stands for independent and circuit operators through the country.

A FRESH APPROACH

After conference with concessionaires and theatre owners in all parts of the country, and after having visited the very latest installations, they sat down with an outstanding young architect, Ira Rakatansky, gave him a layout of the counters and [...]

ternating white and aqua tray rails and point-of-display signs. Pumpkin and yellow have been used to highlight the cocos of the counters. The six 9-foot condiment shelves are pumpkin and white. The interior counters of the work area are aqua with white Formica or stainless steel tops.

Each lane features a Bally ice cream chest especially designed for drive-in theatre use. The tray railing in front of the ice cream fixture is plate glass, giving the customer a free view of the ice cream down in the cabinet. The food department consists of a three-foot radiant unit for buttered popcorn, a four-foot radiant unit which displays regular popcorn, fried clams, shrimp rolls and clam cakes (a product indigenous to Rhode Island), a three-foot Savon Star wet unit for hamburgers, hot dogs, cheeseburgers and steak sandwiches, and a three by four-foot radiant unit for French fries and pizza. The radiant units have been used by the Lowes for ten years and this latest model, as pictured, is the result of many years of development.

The drink department features a stain-

warm months of the year and Orange-CRUSH during the winter season. The backbone of the drink department is a Perlick unit with a special-built Coca-Cola head, which allows a 3½ gallon capacity by means of a pressure system with float valve. Thus the three-drink units dispense Hires root beer, Coca-Cola and Orange-CRUSH during the summer months and when the Orange-CRUSH is moved to the spouter in the winter, it is intended that a still water grape drink be sold as the third flavor of the Perlick unit.

One of the interesting features of the Shipyard Drive-In layout is an individual Cecil five by eight-foot square coffee urn in each lane. A Helmco 12-gallon hot chocolate dispenser will be used in the winter months, positioned between the two coffee urns. Each lane is also equipped with a new Dairy Server electrically operated creamer, which gives the management complete control of the amount of cream used per serving.

The cashiers' booths comfortably hold two cashiers. Three of the cash registers

---

Unusual in design and construction, the three boxoffices, each serving two lanes of traffic, are suspended from a steel overhead canopy. Each boxoffice is painted in a different color pastel.

Section V

HOME BUILDING
REAL ESTATE

The Providence Sund[ay]

PROVIDENCE, R. I., OCTOBER 31

As MODERN as Tomorrow

IN EAST GREENWICH: This house in Modern style was designed by Providence architect Ira Rakatansky for Mr. and Mrs. Sumner B. Halsband. The roof is water-cooled.

ONE WALL of the master bedroom is occupied by ceiling-high closets. Another feature is a bank of drawers with a disappearing built-in desk. The woodwork is birch.

Old East Greenwich Is Setting for New House with Latest Design Features

By DOROTHY AGNEW

RIGHT in the heart of East Greenwich, which probably has more well-preserved 18th- and 19th-century houses to the square foot than any other town in the state, a daring house of modern design has been built.

It is a dwelling that makes no concessions to deeply-implanted old-fashioned ideas. One story high with no basement, it embodies such startling features as a water-cooled roof

with glass brick, at the right of the door.

Corridor From Entrance

From the entrance hall a corridor runs straight ahead into the heart of the house. At the left is a door to the kitchen and just beyond that a door to a heater room which is incorporated in a ceiling-high island between the kitchen and living room.

There is no door where the corridor meets the living room; the two blend. And there is no door between

up new position in the corner or by the dining room.

Like the living room, the kitchen has three white walls and one brown. Doors to all cupboards are natural birch. Counters are dark-brown linoleum. The kitchen also serves as laundry—an automatic washer stands beside the sink counter close to the door leading to the hall.

Storage Wall

Between the living room and a branch of the corridor, from which

---

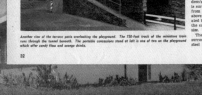

Fireplace opens to all three areas of large family room. Furniture is easy, modern and completely in harmony with its background.

[...]ates over a sunny flagstone terrace — flagstone flooring in large living area

A GOOD PLAN
A GOOD HOUSE

WHEN you walk into this house you have the feeling that its world is young . . . a concentrate of freshness, simplicity, informality. Let's take it apart and analyze it.

Its young family of three wanted spacious, light areas; small secluded bedrooms; and easy to clean finishes. They had no intention of redecorating every few years so they used materials simply . . . materials which would increase in beauty through the years. Wood was left naturally light and waxed flagstones cover the floors serving the rooms from any hint of severity. Outside, too, woods were given a clear weather resistant finish which requires but little upkeep.

As with the house of a hundred years ago, life centers about the fire

everywhere in our country, or a regional cuisine for everybody?"[24] Breuer, picking up on the culinary metaphor, pointed out that the terms 'formal' and 'human' were by no means contradictory, and that modern architecture had never been as doctrinaire in practice as it was in theory, stating, "just as Sullivan did not eat his functionalism as hot as he cooked it, Le Corbusier did not build his machine for living!" At the same time, Breuer declared, "If 'human' is considered identical with redwood all over the place, or if it is considered identical with imperfection and imprecision, I am against it."[25]

In a post-symposium exchange with Barr, Mumford professed that he was bewildered by the depth of misunderstanding of what he had tried to say, and insisted that his 'universal' concept of regionalism could in no way be reduced to "redwood cottage architecture."[26] In fact, the houses of both Wurster and Breuer at this date reflect an authentic appreciation for the local building culture and a humanistic attitude toward living. If Breuer's architecture is far more creative and aesthetically innovative than Wurster's, Wurster's understated, 'everyday' aesthetic of common materials and simplified detailing, his devotion to straightforward construction and functionality, and above all his conception of the 'large-small house' — a small dwelling invested with the quality and livability of one much larger — seem to find a reverberation in the postwar work of Ira Rakatansky.[27] Almost all of Rakatansky's houses manifest a sense of careful aesthetic economy while striving for a feeling of domestic comfort and spatial expansiveness. It might perhaps be said that Rakatansky's work combines aspects of both of these exemplary modernists.[28]

Apropos of the increasingly important discourse on regionalism in the postwar period, it is interesting to note that the Museum of Modern Art's 1940 Guide to Modern Architecture: Northeast States, edited by John McAndrew, included just eight listings for Rhode Island, and only two of them houses.[29] The compendiums of James and Katherine Ford were also lacking in Rhode Island examples, even though their books illustrated a remarkably broad geographic distribution of houses around the United States. (The sole exception was the rather sophisticated and elegantly appointed Dorenbaum House in Providence by Samuel Glaser with L. L. Rado, published in the Fords' 1942 book Design of Modern Interiors.[30])

Henry-Russell Hitchcock's Rhode Island Architecture, a survey of architecture in the state since the seventeenth century, compiled for an exhibition held in 1939 at the art museum of Rhode Island School of Design and curated by Alexander Dorner — another German émigré and a polemical modernist — likewise acknowledged the paucity of significant examples of non-traditional building in Rhode Island to date. In fact, the only modern house that Hitchcock was able to wax enthusiastic about was not even located in Rhode Island: the John Nicholas Brown House on nearby Fisher's Island, New York, designed by the California architect Richard Neutra.[31]

Hitchcock also illustrated a handful of other modern houses in his book, suggesting, however, that although all of them employed a modern formal vocabulary and functionalist planning, they were adaptations of traditional wood-frame construction and as such not dissimilar to the houses crafted by home builders in the seventeenth and eighteenth centuries. Speculating on what the future might hold, he concluded, "Whether we are to have great architects in the mid-twentieth century in America we cannot yet certainly know. But the few houses and factories in [the chapter of the book on modern architecture] give us faith that a vernacular is being established." [32]

The more than fifty houses that Ira Rakatansky constructed in the Providence area as well as elsewhere in Rhode Island and New England in the following few decades – in addition to a complement of synagogues and churches, bowling alleys, drive-in theaters, nurseries, apartment buildings, and other community-oriented and commercial building types – stand as a contribution to the new modern vernacular hopefully augured by Hitchcock. Yet they stood out in their day, and still do, as local exceptions within a surrounding urban or suburban context that has tended to remain mostly conservative and conventional.

An engaging and unusually nuanced inquiry into American architectural habits and taste, written by a member of the architectural profession but reflecting the sociological mindset of the 1950s, is to be found in a book published in 1953 by Robert Woods Kennedy, a Boston-area architect who taught at MIT and was close to Wurster. In *The House and the Art of Its Design*, Kennedy undertook to analyze what type of client was most likely to commission a modern architect to design a house and for what reasons. The 'upper upper' and 'lower upper' classes tended to inherit their wealth and buy older houses with a lineage, according to Kennedy; they employed architects but their taste was conservative and they usually selected architects from their own class. The 'lower middle' class tended to buy speculatively built houses and seldom employed architects; they were 'very conservative' and disliked experimentation. That left the 'upper middle' class, which Kennedy saw as divided into two groups: 'conservative' and 'innovating'. Only the second group, whose members tended to be well educated, socially progressive, and engaged in civic and professional activities, had any real affinity for modern architecture and were likely to hire a modernist architect: "The upper-middle class family in the innovating sub-group is responsible for most of the progress in architecture. It forces the expression of new patterns of living, and of new technical advantage." [33] This, in the author's perhaps overly optimistic calculation, amounted to about five percent of the population.

Kennedy's intuitive class analysis of American domestic preferences and architect-client relations – which also underscores the naiveté of wartime predictions of an emergent classless society in the United States – still seems to hold mostly true more than half a century later. Indeed, it is possible to conclude that the American house has never really been modern, at least not in any popular sense, notwithstanding a few rare moments of enthusiasm. Despite their different levels of affluence, Levitt's Cape Coddages and today's McMansions both reflect a deep-seated attachment to a nostalgic image of home and to a semblance of individuality that is a thinly disguised manifestation of standardized diversity. [34]

In this regard, the houses built by Ira Rakatansky in the postwar decades – those still extant and being comfortably lived in by a third generation of owners, and those only available in archival photographs and construction drawings like the ones in this book – continue to offer a vision of carefully studied, unformulaic, unpretentious, and enlightened living. Economically designed, attuned to their natural environment, and tailored to the needs of their owners, they make the case that the modern house is not a period piece but a continuously fresh approach to contemporary life.

1   "Why I Do Not Live in America," *Transition*, fall 1928; reprinted in Gertrude Stein, *How Writing Is Written*, ed. Robert Bartlett Haas (Los Angeles: Black Sparrow Press, 1974), p 51.

2   Rhode Island School of Design was still a 'trade school'; it did not grant a professional degree in architecture until 1955.

3   Ira Rakatansky in conversation with the author, August 2009.

4   See Anthony Alofsin, *The Struggle for Modernism: Architecture, Landscape Architecture, and City Planning at Harvard* (New York: Norton, 2002), pp 138–248; and especially Jill Pearlman, *Inventing American Modernism: Joseph Hudnut, Walter Gropius, and the Bauhaus Legacy at Harvard* (Charlottesville: University of Virginia Press, 2007), pp 200 ff.

5   Conversation with Ira Rakatansky, August 4, 2009; see also Lynnette Widder's essay in this book.

6   See Pearlman, *Inventing American Modernism*, pp 165–72; Klaus Herdeg, *The Decorated Diagram: Harvard Architecture and the Failure of the Bauhaus Legacy* (Cambridge, MA: MIT Press, 1983), pp 102–3.

7   William H. Jordy, "The Aftermath of the Bauhaus in America: Gropius, Mies, and Breuer," in Donald Fleming and Bernard Bailyn, eds., *Perspectives in American History*, vol. 2, *The Intellectual Migration: Europe and America, 1930–1960* (Cambridge, MA: Charles Warren Center for Studies in American History, 1968), p 522.

8   Ibid., p 523.

9   Ibid., p 491.

10   Russell Lynes, *The Tastemakers* (New York: Harper & Brothers, 1949), pp 248–49.

11   "Design for War," *Architectural Forum*, September 1943, p 4.

12   Robert R. Nathan, *Mobilizing for Abundance* (New York: McGraw-Hill, 1944); "What Happened to the Dreamworld?" *Fortune*, February 1947, p 93.

13   *Pencil Points*, September 1945, p 59.

14   Roland Marchand, "Visions of Classlessness, Quests for Dominion: American Popular Culture, 1945–1960," in Robert H. Bremner and Gary W. Reichard, eds., *Reshaping America: Society and Institutions, 1945–1960* (Columbus: Ohio State University Press, 1982), p 164.

15   The architects and designers in the Revere series included Norman Bel Geddes, George Nelson, Paul Nelson, Walter Dorwin Teague, Buckminster Fuller, George Fred Keck, William Wurster, William Lescaze, Oscar Stonorov and Louis Kahn, Serge Chermayeff, Antonin Raymond, and others. Similar advertising campaigns featuring houses by modern architects were carried out by companies like Celotex, Monsanto, U.S. Gypsum, Timken Silent Automatic, and Pittsburgh Plate Glass. On the relationship between wartime advertising and architecture, see a recent book by Andrew M. Shanken: *194X: Architecture, Planning, and Consumer Culture on the American Home Front* (Minneapolis: University of Minnesota Press, 2009).

16   Elizabeth Mock, *If You Want to Build a House* (New York: Museum of Modern Art, 1946). "An attitude towards life," p 7.

17   George Nelson and Henry Wright, *Tomorrow's House: How to Plan Your Post-War House Now* (New York: Simon and Schuster, 1945), p 139.

18   James Ford and Katherine Morrow Ford, *The Modern House in America* (New York: Architectural Book Publishing Co., 1940), p 8. This book contains an interesting appendix on "America's Contribution to Modern Architecture," in which the architects whose houses were included in the volume were asked to provide a statement "indicating at what points American work in modern design and construction departs from European methods and may be termed distinctively American"; pp 123–29.

19   "WHY Is a Modern House?" *Splendor*, April 1949, pp 14–15.

20   Lynes, *The Tastemakers*, p 250.

21   Lewis Mumford, "The Skyline: Status Quo," *New Yorker*, October 11, 1947, p 110.

22   Catherine Bauer to Lewis Mumford, letter of January 29, 1932; cited in Terence Riley, ed., *The International Style: Exhibition 15 and the Museum of Modern Art* (New York: Rizzoli, 1992), p 209.

23   Mumford, "The Skyline: Status Quo," p 110.

24   "What Is Happening to Modern Architecture? A Symposium at the Museum of Modern Art," *Museum of Modern Art Bulletin*, spring 1948, p 12.

25   Ibid., p 15.

26   Ibid., p 21.

27   On Wurster's "everyday modernism," see Marc Treib, ed., *An Everyday Modernism: The Houses of William Wurster* (Berkeley: San Francisco Museum of Modern Art and University of California Press, 1995); and R. Thomas Hille, *Inside the Large Small House: The Residential Design Legacy of William W. Wurster* (Ann Arbor, Michigan, 1994).

28   It is worth mentioning that Richard Neutra is the architect whom Rakatansky most admires. In later years he had the opportunity to visit the work of Le Corbusier, Gaudí, and other European architects; he appreciated their work but says they were not influential for him. Conversation with Ira Rakatansky, August 2009.

29   John McAndrew, ed., *Guide to Modern Architecture: Northeast States* (New York: Museum of Modern Art, 1940). The two houses listed are the Donnelly house at Plum Beach by George Howe and Robert Montgomery Brown, 1938; and Alexander Knox's house for himself in Saunderstown, 1935, addition 1938.

30   James Ford and Katherine Morrow Ford, *Design of Modern Interiors* (New York: Architectural Book Publishing Company, 4th ed., 1945), pp 27, 30, 78.

31   Henry-Russell Hitchcock, Jr., *Rhode Island Architecture* (Cambridge, MA: MIT Press, 1968; republication of first edition published in 1939 by Rhode Island Museum Press), p 66, plates 73–74. Hitchcock justified including the Neutra house on the grounds that the owner was from an important Rhode Island family. Neutra was, of course, another émigré modernist, and one of the earliest, having arrived in the United States from Austria in the 1920s.

32   Ibid., p 69. The other modern houses that appear in the book are the Donnelly and Knox houses, also listed in McAndrew's guidebook (see note 28); Norman Herreshoff's house for himself in Bristol, 1938; and the Mary Ellis house in East Greenwich by William and Sylvia Wilde, 1938–39. Hitchcock also includes one example of prefabricated housing, the Nicholas Monsarrat and Jane Monsarrat Houses in East Providence, by the General Housing Corporation, 1936.

33   See Robert Woods Kennedy, *The House and the Art of Its Design* (New York: Reinhold, 1953), pp 16–21.

34   On the concept of standardized diversity, see Stuart Ewen, *All Consuming Images: The Politics of Style in Contemporary Culture* (New York: Basic Books, 1988), p 229. Ewen attributes the origin of this concept to American architects like Walter Dorwin Teague, Alfred T. North, and Randolph Evans in the 1930s and '40s. Evans, a pioneer of suburban tract communities, argued in *Architectural Record* in 1944 that crews applying a factory approach to housing construction could produce as many as seventy-two 'surface variations' on a single floor plan.

Construction Transparency
Lynnette Widder

The transposition of architecture from idea to realization is subject to a much larger degree of uncertainty than most of us would like to think. The act of producing an architectural work also marks the beginning of the act of its reception, through the medium of the drawing as a directive, rather than descriptive, tool. Architecture's first audience is the people involved in the construction process. The architect, who as a rule does not physically produce his or her own work, is charged with developing the ability to see, viscerally, through the drawings to the other side, to the process of the work's actualization as it becomes physical reality. At their most powerful, drawings intended to be used in the realization of architecture are transparent: they are legible directives to construction sequence, three-dimensional reality, division of labor and sensual experience, all at once. To look from this perspective at the working drawings produced in the office of Ira Rakatansky— the actual authorial attri- bution of each drawing is unimportant, since the consistency of hand, sensibility and content is more deserving of comment— is a source of real pleasure. Rakatansky's knowledge of building con- struction dates from childhood memories of working in summer at his father's construction sites, collecting nails dropped by carpenters in the course of the day. He attributes to his father, a speculative builder of typical Providence 'triple-decker' houses, and to his aunt, a seamstress who explained to him the relationship between two-dimensional representation and three-dimensional volumetric development by means of pattern-making, the roots of his interest in architecture.[1] His later studies, from 1943 to 1946, at the Harvard University Graduate School of Design with Marcel Breuer, Hugh Stubbins and Walter Gropius, corresponded to a moment in which developments in American building construction were being integrated into the definition of an emergent American High Modernist idiom. As Breuer's first employee in his small Cambridge office, developing the drawing sets for the Geller House of 1945, he deployed directly his talent for the integration of construction thinking into the architecture's spatial and material conception. The drawing sets for Rakatansky's own built projects, beginning in 1947, evidence the fluency with which he moved among the components of architecture: from abstract space to material to construction labor to the life which would inhabit the completed building.

Three case studies drawn from Rakatansky's career from the mid-1940s to the early 1960s describe precisely what is meant by 'construction transparency'. In each case, the drawings' transparency reveals the intended built work, of course, but also snippets of biography, social context, construction habits, economic status, architectural ideology, lifestyle and any number of other possible inferences that inhere to a rich, legible historical document.

1   Interview, Lynnette Widder with Ira Rakatansky, October 31, 2005, in Providence.

CONTINUES IN THREE PARTS ON PAGES 35, 60, 182

Selected Works
1944–1964

Thief River Falls Library Addition 1944

Produced for a studio class with
Marcel Breuer just prior to Rakatansky's Bachelor of Architecture
thesis, this project for a library
addition, sited in Minnesota, is one
of the rare examples in Rakatansky's extensive archive of perspective and presentation-only
drawings. The fine delineation of
texture and detail in the plans indicate his respect for drawing as a
craft. The subtle rendition in perspective of plants at the large glass
façade suggests his interest in an
intimate relationship between
interior and nature even in a harsh
climate. This interest persists in
Rakatansky's first independent
commission, the Halsband House.
Other indications of future interests
are evident in the large fireplace
used to suggest a spatial subdivision and in the choice of plywood,
fieldstone and brick as finishes.

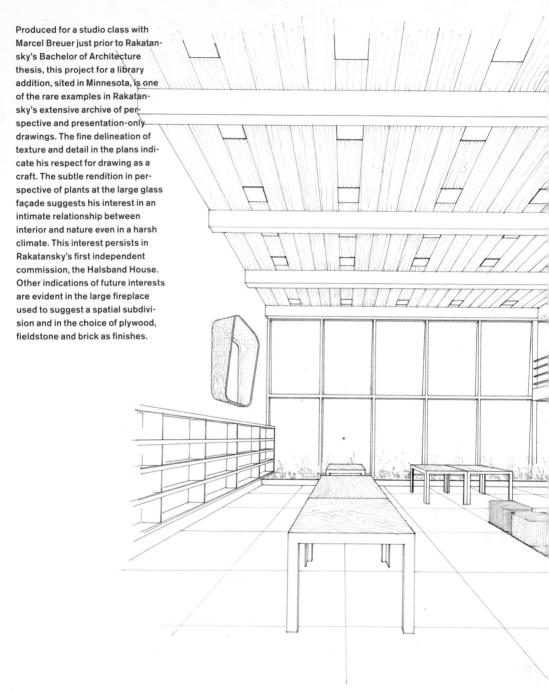

In August of 1944, Rakatansky's second year as a
Bachelor of Architecture student at the GSD,
Marcel Breuer offered a '2c' pre-thesis level design
studio to consider a small library addition to a neoclassical building in Thief River Falls, "(pop 6,019)
… approximately 96–12′ West longitude, 48–8′
North latitude, in the State of Minnesota…."[2]
Breuer's text describes the community wryly, as
"mid-western Republicans … a shrewd people, fond
of family, of good food, and of driving a hard bar-
gain. They are generally careful of their own money
and of the public funds." The addition to the existing 1917 library was to support the librarian's wish
"to make the library a dynamic force for education
in the community," to "welcome any practical sug-
gestions, however 'untraditional'," and to express
being "much interested in modern design." Otherwise, the project brief includes a description of
required program, a simple site drawing and a post-
card of the existing masonry building. At that time,
it was GSD practice to retain photostatic records of
several student projects; in this case, as in several
others during Rakatansky's studies at the GSD, his
work was chosen for documentation. This project
seems also to have had particular importance to
Rakatansky, whose personal archive includes the
original submission drawings with one notable
exception: the required page of construction
details. By odd coincidence, the archived copy of
Breuer's syllabus also does not include the page
listing submission requirements, among them the
construction details.

Construction knowledge figured large in Rakatansky's experience at the GSD. He recalls his first
and only day in Hugh Stubbins' class, "Materials
and Methods of Architectural Construction,"

offered in the second and third years of the Bachelor of Architecture degree program as "a study of basic construction technique and its relation to design."[3] He had set up his drafting board and begun to draw the first assignment. Stubbins, walking around the room to observe the students' work, paused at Rakatansky's drawing, then asked his name. "Rakatansky," he said, "you can leave. You don't need to take this course."[4] Implicit in Stubbins' confidence was not only the fact that Rakatansky's construction experience had provided him with adequate knowledge, but also — given the course's explicit intent – the recognition that Rakatansky had already understood how to deploy that knowledge in the service of an architectural idea.

Thereafter, his classmates looked to him for advice in the area of building construction.[5] Rakatansky also recalls vividly an animated exchange with Walter Gropius, whom he remembers as otherwise reserved: While working on his Bachelor of Architecture thesis in 1946, Rakatansky had chosen a desk in the same room as Gropius' master class. One evening, shortly before he left for the day, Gropius stopped to look at Rakatansky's project for a synagogue in Providence. To shade the main sanctuary from southern light, Rakatansky was developing a louver system using standard aluminum extrusions but had not yet perfected his proposal. Gropius returned the next morning with a series of his own studies of the detail problem. While Gropius's appreciation of the thesis project is underscored by the fact that he later recommended it for publication,[6] his investment in a single construction detail attests to the importance given to construction relative to design at the GSD, and in particular, to the timeliness of the problem Rakatansky was studying: the deployment of highly expedient but not clearly culturally connoted American construction practice within a culturally valued space.

The issue of cultural connotation resonates also in the project statement circulated by Breuer for the library addition project, and is likewise reflected in the details of the primary entry façade, chosen for representation in the archived student projects. Three well-detailed projects by Rakatansky and two fellow students bear out this interest in an appropriately civic application of new construction conditions; they also bear out the idea that construction decisions are transparent to both the architecture intended and the author of the drawing.

By all accounts, the group of students with whom Rakatansky studied during the war years was very heterogeneous,[7] including women, foreign students, African Americans, Jews and others who might not have attended in the earlier years of exclusionary, if not by today's standards discriminatory, admission practices; many went on to assume significant roles in their own rights, if not with the prominence achieved by such famous near-contemporaries as I. M. Pei, Philip Johnson or Paul Rudolph. Two of Rakatansky's fellow students in Breuer's studio were, like Rakatansky, non-traditional to Harvard undergraduate education: Theodore Jan Prichard, an established Beaux-Arts architect educated in Minnesota who later served for 39 years as Dean of the College of Art and Architecture at University of Idaho; and Basil Yurchenco, an Argentine painter of Russian descent who received a degree from Yale in 1935, contributed to the Connecticut WPA painting program and, subsequent to graduation, was partner in a prolific architectural office in New York specialized in commercial and health care buildings. Rakatansky, Prichard and Yurchenco are included in Breuer's archive of letters, and all

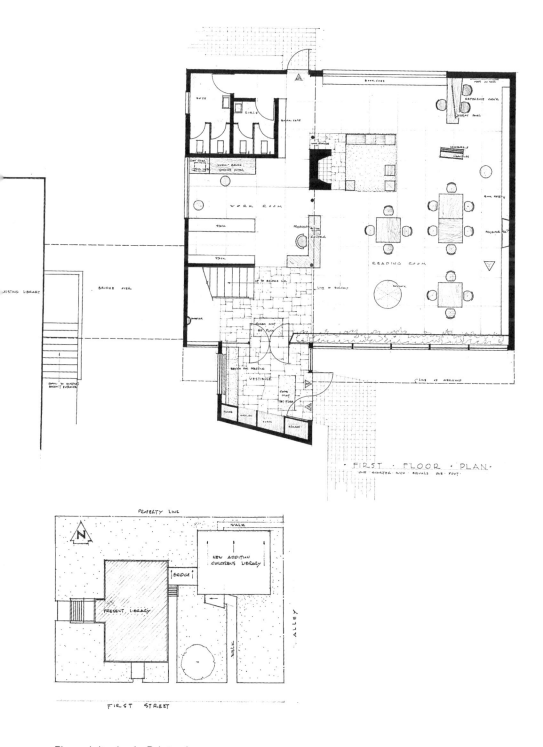

Plan and site plan, Ira Rakatansky

arrived at Harvard with established career paths.[8]

It is fair to assume that Yurchenco arrived at the GSD with the least architectural knowledge among the three classmates, an assumption drawn less from sketchy biographical material than from the way he rendered building construction. Yurchenco's drawing is that of someone who knows construction as an academic subject: a radiator, the lock at the bottom left corner of the glass entry door and the cross-bracing between ceiling joists are drawn precisely, although they are all secondary to the transmission of information needed by the people who might be charged with building the structure. At the same time, the vital detail at the intersection between a low concrete shell entry and the double height glass façade with awning clerestory windows is glossed over. The project's architectural challenge – to position a deep roof, shown as wood framed, atop tapered ribs which act both as window mullions and as stabilizing members for the precast concrete entry element – is left unresolved. Instead, the larger detail provided is banal, if correctly drawn: the juncture between the lally column which carries the roof load, so that the large glass façade can remain thin and unburdened by structural demands, and the conventional wood roof construction. Designations, stipples, hatching are alibis; this is not a drawing which could assume authority at the construction site.

At the same time, there is much to be learned from the drawing about the way architecture's relation to building was taught at the GSD. An earlier Modernist rhetoric of 'truth in material expression' seems to have been reframed in favor of architectural expression to which material and construction choices were subordinate. The very powerful gesture of the ribbed, cast concrete entry volume, elevated above ground level on a cantilevered concrete plane, is placed against the slender, wispy 'curtain' of glass – reinforced by the 'glass woven curtains' specified in the drawing just behind the curtain wall – which spans below the heavy roof. It is easy to imagine this juxtaposition of volumetric concrete entry and planarly defined reading room behind it; the tapered ribs in the entry and the curtain wall belong to an emerging tendency towards mannered delicacy and splined corners typical of much post-war Modernism in the US.

Prichard's detail drawing represents perhaps the opposite extreme in terms of both construction knowledge and architectural expression. This drawing could easily have been part of a bid set generated by a well-run architectural office, with appropriate details called out, products specified, custom elements noted and building materials sized. Prichard even went so far as to specify catalogue furniture in his perspective drawings. The project's expression is more direct than Yuchenco's intended subtle play of volume and plane in which each elements' relative delicacy or depth was decisive: Prichard proposed a solid masonry shell with one large glazed opening set back from the edge of the cantilevered concrete roof edge, coplanar with the edge of the primary volume. The mezzanine level, cleverly supported between the heavy fireplace wall on the right and a 3″ pipe suspending it from the primary roof structure on the left, halves the height of the main space and bisects it symmetrically in plan. Prichard's architectural skill is evident in the progression from double height glass wall, shaded by the overhang to retain its transparency, to the modestly scaled wood-clad space beneath the mezzanine to the volumetric and material presence of the large fireplace wall to the simple, white-tiled, dimmer space behind the fireplace

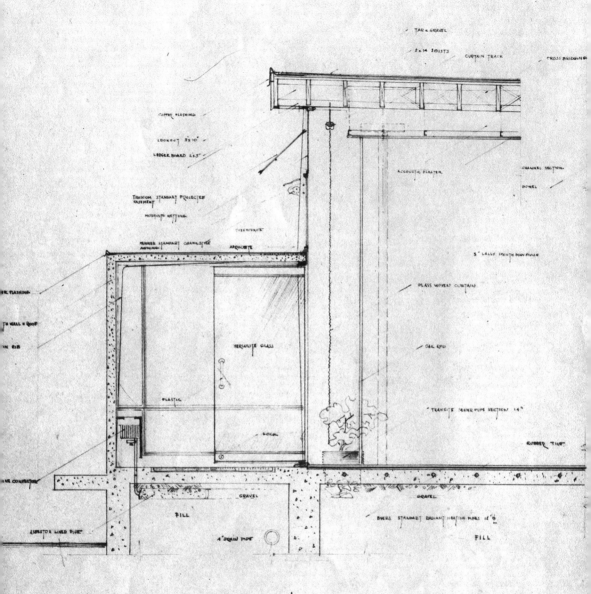

TAR & GRAVEL

2x14 JOISTS

CURTAIN TRACK

CROSS BRIDGING

COPPER FLASHING

LOOKOUT 3x10"

LEDGER BOARD 2x3"

ACOUSTIC PLASTER

CHANNEL SECTION

DOWEL

TRUSCON STANDART PROJECTED
CASEMENT

MOSQUITO NETTING

5" LALLY SMOOTH DOOR FINISH

THERMOPANE

PENNER STANDART CRANK-TYPE
AWNING

ARBOCITE

GLASS WOVEN CURTAIN

HERCULITE GLASS

OAK END

PLASTIC

"TRANSITE SEWER PIPE SECTION 14"

LUCAL

RUBBER TILE

WALL FLASHING

WALL & ROOF

CRIB

VANE CONNECTOR

GRAVEL

GRAVEL

FILL

BYERS STANDART RADIANT HEATING PIPES 1" Ø

ASBESTOS LINED PIPE

4" DRAIN PIPE

FILL

SECTION B-B'

Detail section, Basil Yurchenco

wall. He has produced a beautifully drafted, articulate drawing, which speaks to his architectural intention and to its competent realization.

In terms of detailing and spatial sensibility, Prichard's project could be said to represent the adaptation of American architectural and construction culture to a Modern idiom. The products called for, from hollow structural clay tile to linoleum to deep, pressed steel window mullions to acoustical tile, are state of the art in technological terms, but stylistically neutral in terms of expression, as much at home in the Beaux-Arts Neo-Gothic gymnasium on which Prichard had worked as project and construction manager prior to coming to the GSD,[9] as in an Art Deco or Modern context. The carefully staged sequence from high to low, light to dark, transparent to solid, relates as much to the staged, sequential parti of the Beaux-Arts tradition as to the ideal of flowing, ambiguously bounded space inherent to a Modernist sensibility.

Rakatansky's drawing is one of an architect used to moving quickly and expediently from conception to construction: well-drawn and laid-out, it nonetheless breaks the building into a series of significant detail moments independent of their coherence in the space as a whole. Although by no means less accurate or authoritative than Prichard's drawing in terms of the sizing or designation of materials and members, Rakatansky's does not demand particular products. The attitude toward specification is one that fits comfortably in framed building practice, in which standard components are easily modified to make such unusual elements as the light baffles shown in the right hand wall section or the tapered look-out shown in the roof details which intelligently slopes away from the main entry façade to the building's back, shedding water to

a tried and true gutter but giving the appearance of a flat roof with none of its complications. It is a hybrid of component-based and bespoke construction, in which convention coexists with such non-traditional details as the recessed baseboard, a detail favored by Rakatansky even now. It is also the drawing of an architect who knew the limits of what could be determined in a document, and what needed to be dictated on site in order to be effective.

The choice of wood construction for a public building is in marked contrast to both Prichard's and Yuchenco's approaches. Rakatansky's decision to sheath the building in 6″ vertical siding, the use of cork tile above radiant heat pipes in a simple concrete slab, the narrow roof edge achieved only with flashing and tar paper, the deployment of a simple lally column as dictated by spatial need all presage the vocabulary of the small, precise houses he would be building soon after this project was completed. They also relate directly to the New England Modernism that Breuer and Gropius had begun to develop in their collaborative and individual house projects, and which was further expounded by their colleagues at the GSD.[10]

2   Breuer's syllabus is preserved in the Special Collections of the Frances Loeb Library, Harvard University GSD. According to D. Nels Reese, Theodore Jan Prichard's biographer, Thief River Falls is the birthplace of Rakatansky's classmate. The prose in which the syllabus is written recalls Prichard's writing. Prichard, who was 42 and had returned to Harvard to finish his master's thesis after a thirteen-year hiatus, is likely to have contributed to the problem statement. Conversation between D. Nels Reese and LW, August 17, 2009.

3   A comparison between the GSD course catalogues from 1936–37 and 1944–45 reveals a clear movement towards the greater integration of construction technologies into the architectural curriculum in those years. The 1936 curriculum includes only one course in Building Construction, footnoted to indicate that it is among the courses "required only of students who have not included them in their college course." (1936 *Official Register of Harvard University*, p 23). The 1944 curriculum stipulates two full years of Stubbins' Materials and Methods course, as well as 'Construction Drawing' taught by Jean Georges

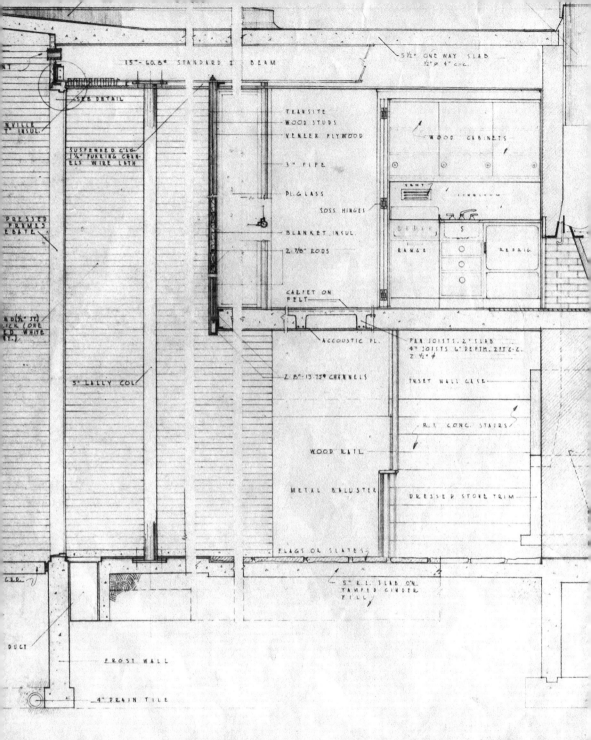

15"- 60.8# STANDARD I BEAM

5½" ONE WAY SLAB
½" Ø 4" C=C=

SEE DETAIL

NVILLE
T' INSUL.

TRANSITE
WOOD STUDS
VENEER PLYWOOD

WOOD CABINETS

SUSPENDED C'IG
1¾" FURRING CHAN-
ELS WIRE LATH

3" PIPE

PRESSED
FRAMES
EBATE

PL. GLASS

VENT   LINOLEUM

SOSS HINGES

BLANKET INSUL.

FRIG.

RANGE   S   REFRIG.

2- ⅞" RODS

R D (½" 5T)
ICK (ONE
E D. WHITE
1"L)

CARPET ON
FELT

ACCOUSTIC PL.

PAN JOISTS. 2" SLAB
4" JOISTS 6" DEPTH. 2FT C-C.
2 ½" Ø

5" LALLY COL.

2- 8"- 13.75# CHANNELS

INSET WALL CASE

R.I. CONC. STAIRS

WOOD RAIL

METAL BALUSTER

DRESSED STONE TRIM

FLAGS OR SLATES

5" R.I. SLAB ON
TAMPED CINDER
FILL

RED

DUCT

FROST WALL

4" DRAIN TILE

COMPOSITE SECTION.   TYPICAL & SPECIAL DETAILS

Detail section, Theodore Jan Prichard

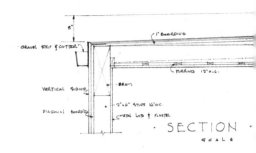

· SECTION ·

Peter and two Design Studios (Architecture 4a in the first year and Architecture 2b in the second year) that were titled 'Architecture Design and Building Construction'. Although the building construction syllabi were not archived with the design work in Frances Loeb Library, the exercises given and the way in which standard construction techniques and specifiable products were treated merits attention. The 1944 catalogue's description of Stubbins' course implies a close understanding of the changing relationship between construction on site and the fabrication of building parts elsewhere: "This course is a study of basic construction technique and its relation to design. It is conducted through: (a) field trips to familiarize students with the problems of and good practice in *construction and with the fabrication and construction of building parts*; (b) lectures, demonstrations, and reading on procedure in construction development of ideas into *practical working details and specifications*, including color, texture, durability, selection, and installation of materials; (c) class exercises to develop a knowledge of the principles of good detailing and drafting technique. [italics LW]" (*The Graduate School of Design Description of the Courses in Architecture, Landscape Architecture and Planning*, 1944–45, p 32).

4   Rakatansky, in conversation. He has repeated this story on several occasions in discussions of his studies at the GSD.

5   Rakatansky recalls sitting near Anne Tyng while she was working on her thesis project, a house for her parents, and having conversations with her about its construction. Rakatansky in conversation, August 4, 2009.

6   The project was published in *Progressive Architecture* in December of 1945; see p 46 of this book.

7   See Jill Pearlman, *Inventing American Modernism: Joseph Hudnut, Walter Gropius and the Bauhaus Legacy at Harvard* (University of Virginia Press: Charlottesville and London, 2007), p 200; also, in conversation with Ira Rakatansky and Joan Ockman, August 4, 2009.

8   See Marcel Breuer Papers – Collection Online – Archives of American Art – Smithsonian Institution: Series 2, Reel 5712, Frame 210 and 211 (Rakatansky); Reel 5711, Frame 406 ff and 447 (Yurchenco); and Reel 5711, Frames 409 and 445 (Prichard).

9   As described by D. Nels Reese, who is preparing a professional biography of Theodore Jan Prichard. The drawings for this 1927 building on University of Idaho campus in Moscow are part of an online archive; see supernova.dfm.uidaho.edu/A/103/015-MGYM-Originals.pdf. My thanks to Mr. Reese for sharing his information and insights.

10 See, for example, Pearlman, Op. Cit., pp 112–118.

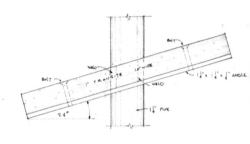

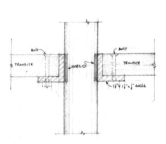

· DETAIL · OF · LOUVRE ·

Detail sections, Ira Rakatansky

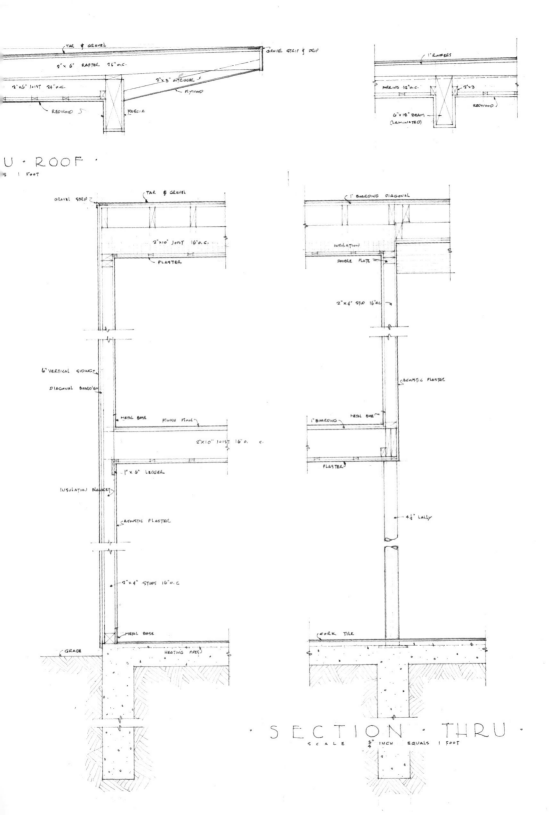

TAR & GRAVEL
2" x 6" RAFTER 16" O.C.
GRAVEL STRIP & DRIP
2"x6" JOIST 24"O.C.
2"x3" OUTRIGGER
PLYWOOD
REDWOOD S
FASCIA

1" RAFTERS
PURLINS 12"O.C.
2"x3
REDWOOD
6"x18" BEAM
(LAMINATED)

U · ROOF ·
S 1 FOOT

GRAVEL STRIP
TAR & GRAVEL
1" BOARDING DIAGONAL
2"x10" JOIST 16"O.C.
PLASTER
INSULATION
DOUBLE PLATE
2"x4" STUD 16"O.C.
6" VERTICAL SIDING
DIAGONAL BOARD'G
METAL BASE
FINISH FLOOR
ACOUSTIC PLASTER
2"X10" JOIST 16"O. C.
METAL BASE
1" BOARDING
1" x 6" LEDGER
PLASTER
INSULATION BLANKET
ACOUSTIC PLASTER
4¼" LALLY
2"x4" STUDS 16"O.C
METAL BASE
CORK TILE
GRADE
HEATING PIPES

· SECTION · THRU ·
SCALE ¾" INCH EQUALS 1 FOOT

Reform Temple Thesis Project 1945

For his Bachelor of Architecture thesis, Rakatansky developed a speculative project based upon a newspaper item he had found, which announced the purchase by the reform Jewish congregation of a building lot on Providence's historic East Side. Although he does not practice any religion, Rakatansky has remained fascinated by the possibility of 'sacred space' throughout his career and is the architect of several sacral buildings. The project's sober layout, which locates school and sanctuary around the entry foyer, produces expressive massing, in which each functional element is evident within the balanced composition of wall, strip window and the operable louvers, which shade the sanctuary from southern light.

The level of detail, including lighting design, sliding door detail, footing detail and handrail design, evidences Rakatansky's exceptional ability to draw upon his construction knowledge to support an architectural concept. Upon the recommendation of Walter Gropius, with whom Rakatansky completed his Master of Architecture one year later, the project was published in an issue of *Progressive Architecture* dedicated to religious buildings. A synagogue was ultimately built on this site by Percival Goodman in 1954.

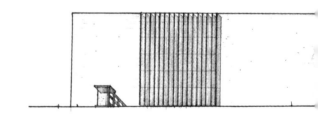

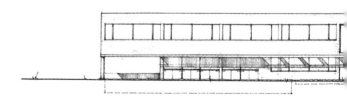

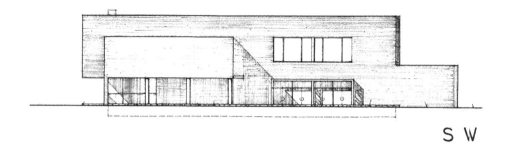

S W

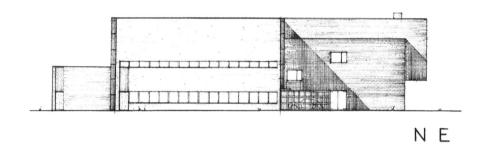

N E

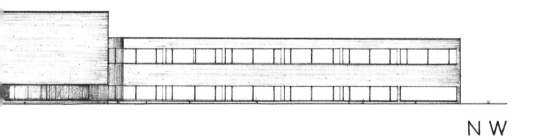

N W

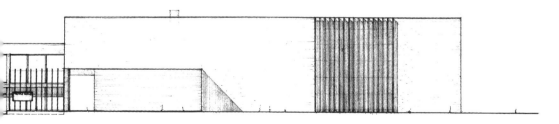

S E

Problem: To design a Reform Temple for an actual Providence, R. I., congregation and a site of 88,609 square feet. The designer lists the requirements as follows: a Temple (auditorium for 800, rabbi's study, etc.); a Chapel (for small weddings and daily services) to seat 100; and a Meeting House, including religious school rooms, a nursery, a gymnasium-dance hall—dining room, the Temple offices, and a library.

Solution: The three major elements are arranged around and entered from a central courtyard. Both Synagogue and Chapel face east (according to tradition) and are directly served (without stair climbing) from the main doors. The court is also useful as an off-sidewalk gathering place after services.

A thoughtful provision is the coat-checking room at the entrance to the Synagogue. To accommodate crowds on high holidays, a lifting partition is provided at the rear of the main auditorium balcony. The kitchen is placed so that it serves both the ground floor rooms and (by means of a dumb-waiter) the upstairs social hall.

Construction: The proposed structural system is a steel frame with concrete rib floor slabs and 12-inch masonry filler walls, except in the Chapel where a two-way pan concrete slab on a masonry bearing wall is used. For heating, the proposal is to use a split system—panel heat for the first floor slabs and on the side walls of the main auditorium and the Chapel, supplemented by a blower to circulate air in the auditoriums. In summer cold water would be circulated in the floor panels. Convectors are specified for the second floor. Fixed, structural fins outside the large windows of the main auditorium are arranged for favorable daylight control.

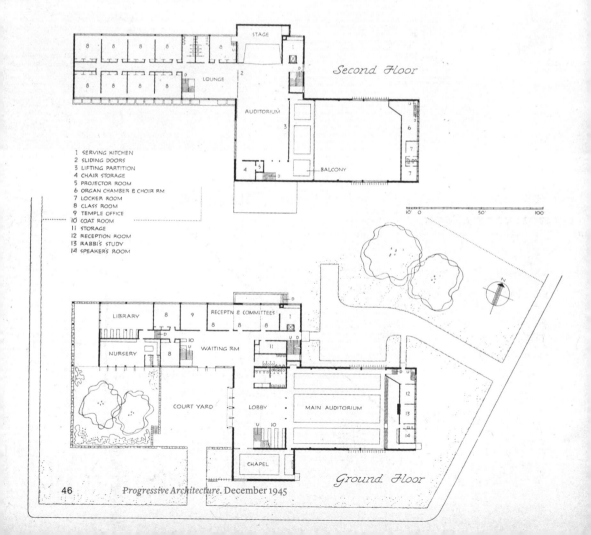

1 SERVING KITCHEN
2 SLIDING DOORS
3 LIFTING PARTITION
4 CHAIR STORAGE
5 PROJECTOR ROOM
6 ORGAN CHAMBER & CHOIR RM
7 LOCKER ROOM
8 CLASS ROOM
9 TEMPLE OFFICE
10 COAT ROOM
11 STORAGE
12 RECEPTION ROOM
13 RABBI'S STUDY
14 SPEAKER'S ROOM

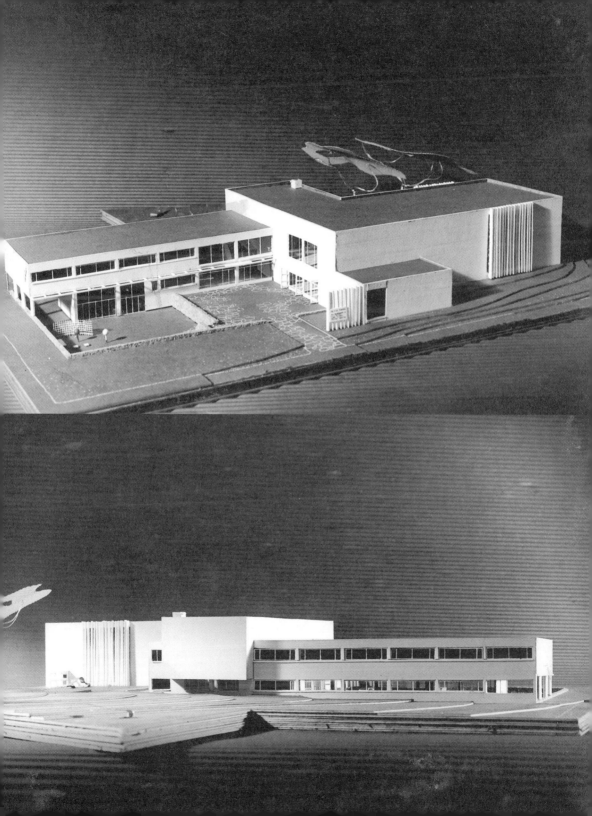

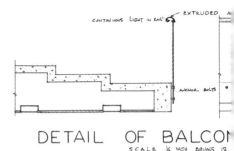

DETAIL OF BALCON
SCALE ½ INCH EQUALS 12

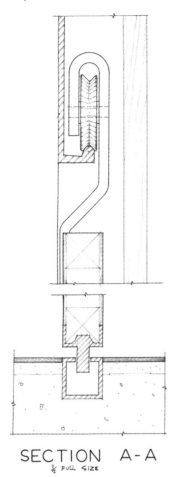

SECTION A-A
½ FULL SIZE

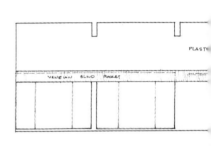

ELEVATION SHOWIN
SCALE ⅛ INCH E

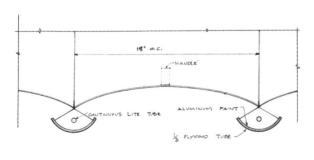

LIGHTING 3 INCHES EQUALS 12

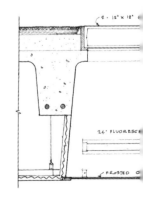

SKYLIG

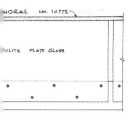

NDRAIL   No. 10772

ULITE   PLATE GLASS

ANDRAIL

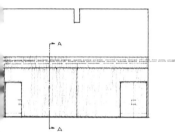

A

A

DING   DOORS

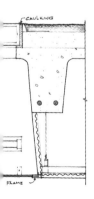

CAULKING

FRAME

CHES   EQUALS   12

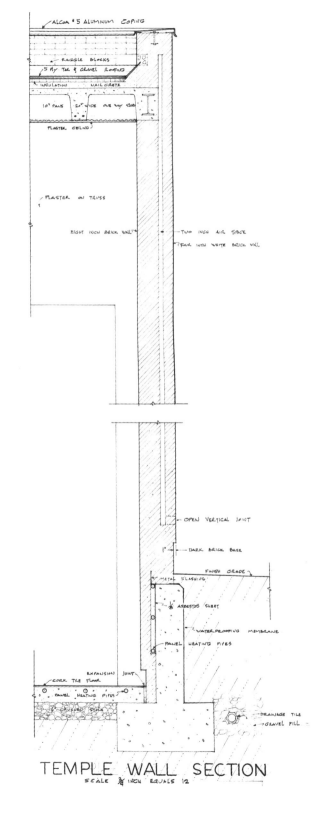

ALCOA #5 ALUMINUM COPING

RAGGLE BLOCKS

5 PLY TAR & GRAVEL ROOFING

INSULATION   NAILCRETE

10" PANS   20" WIDE ONE WAY SLAB

PLASTER CEILING

PLASTER ON TRUSS

EIGHT INCH BRICK WALL

TWO INCH AIR SPACE

FOUR INCH WHITE BRICK WALL

OPEN VERTICAL JOINT

1"   DARK BRICK BASE

FINISH GRADE

METAL FLASHING

ASBESTOS SHEET

WATERPROOFING MEMBRANE

PANEL HEATING PIPES

EXPANSION JOINT

CORK TILE FLOOR

PANEL HEATING PIPES

CRUSHED STONE

DRAINAGE TILE

GRAVEL FILL

TEMPLE   WALL   SECTION
SCALE 3/8 INCH EQUALS 12

Halsband House 1947

The Halsband House is located on Proctor Avenue in East Greenwich, Rhode Island. It was designed for Rakatansky's sister and built in collaboration with his father.

The flat-roofed one-story house is compact, with only two bedrooms. The plan is structured around the central utility room containing a boiler and hot water heater, which also serves as a back wall to the ceiling-height fireplace in the living room. Floor-to-ceiling doorways support the reading of space as continuous, even in the wing of the building occupied by the bedrooms. All rooms are defined by planes and volumes, not by walls with openings. Rather than specify custom doors, Rakatansky used a standard sized door for the lower portion of each opening, and another door panel cut in half for the upper portion, creating a 'reverse Dutch door' which operates much like a transom for ventilation. Every detail is considered, such as the flush alignment of the glass bead in the entry transom to the width of the doorframe. Rakatansky designed the house's freestanding bookcase and the rest of the furniture. The role this furniture plays in spatial definition justifies this care; as Rakatansky describes it, if the scale of the furniture is off, it is "like seeing a serving apron being worn over a wedding gown."

Flagstone flooring in entire main living
area of house (main passage at left and
living room below and across-page) plus
radiant heat in the floor slab makes it
possible to clean the house "in less than
an hour."

LINE OF ROOF ABOVE

LIVING ROOM

BEDROOM

DINING

HEAT

BATH

KITCHEN

NURSERY

ENTRY

Floor Plan   Scale 0   5′   10′

program	An easy-to-maintain house having two bedrooms, a living room wi dining area, a kitchen, and a bath.
site	A 75′ x 100′ corner lot. Space for future garage and enclosed stora room.
solution	Compact plan, within a simple rectangle; central entrance; main livi space organized around an interior boiler-service room; two bedroo and bath at right of passageway. For efficient housekeeping, sla flagstone is used for flooring in the living space, bath, and kitche asphalt tile in the bedrooms.

program An easy-to-maintain house having two bedrooms, a living room wi dining area, a kitchen, and a bath.

site A 75′ x 100′ corner lot. Space for future garage and enclosed stora room.

solution Compact plan, within a simple rectangle; central entrance; main livi space organized around an interior boiler-service room; two bedroo and bath at right of passageway. For efficient housekeeping, sla flagstone is used for flooring in the living space, bath, and kitche asphalt tile in the bedrooms.

materials and methods CONSTRUCTION: *Foundation:* concrete. *Frame:* wood. *Walls:* wo stud, surfaced on the exterior with ⅜″ waterproof, scored plywo (painted); inside, with hard lime plaster, except in the bathroo (scored plywood) and the boiler room (asbestos cement board). *Floo* concrete slab, surfaced with either flagging or asphalt tile. *Roofin* tar and gravel over wood rafters and decking. *Insulation:* 1″ boa type in roof; aluminum reflective material in the walls. *Fenestratio* steel sash; plate glass.

EQUIPMENT: *Heating:* radiant system in floor slab; copper tubing; fuel; controls. *Lighting:* both incandescent and fluorescent.

the designer *Ira Rakatansky:* Rhode Island School of Design; B. Arch., and Arch., Harvard Graduate School of Design. Work in the offices of M cel Breuer and Samuel M. Morino.

Caption

The uptake by the building industry of plywood after the invention of water-resistant glues in the mid-1930s was slowed only by the weak building economy during the Depression. Although Rhode Island's boat building industry and the important Navy installation at Quonset may have contributed to a wider-spread use of plywood in that state than elsewhere, it is certain that Ira Rakatansky's father, Benjamin, used light timber frames sheathed only in diagonal boards on the exterior, and wood lathe with horsehair plaster on the interior to construct the triple deckers on which his son worked before and during his studies at Harvard.[11] Although low material cost was part of balloon framing's appeal, the labor pool in Providence was equally signifi-cant. Immigrant construction workers – in the 1940s, largely Italians and French Canadians – could install plaster at a speed comparable to early dry construction, favoring older techniques over the labor-saving but material-cost-intensive technology of plywood and the tools needed to use it. Many carpenters were Swedish, and brought with them the skill and knowledge to build the more complicated balloon frame structure, with its notched floor joists and intercut primary connections.[12]

By his own account, Rakatansky first began to include plywood in his detailing repertoire shortly after earning his Master of Architecture from the GSD in 1946, while collaborating with the engineer Samuel Lerner before establishing his independent practice.[13] His stated reasons for choosing the material are not ideological but rather straightfor-ward. He first saw plywood used on job sites for foundations as part of construction practice rather than architect's specifications. Where contractors had formerly used boards for formwork, which were then reused as sheathing or subfloor, they began to use plywood which they also reused elsewhere. This early plywood was coarse and difficult to cut evenly, especially since the appropriate tools for cutting it on site were not yet commonplace.[14] At a point soon thereafter, he recalls, he had in his office material library a full assortment of avail-able plywood cores and veneers, which he used in specifying the material. Especially for built-in cabinetry, simple Douglas Fir and birch ply – some-times painted but most often simply sealed with a clear varnish – became a significant component in what Rakatansky has referred to as the 'music' of materials which together comprise a harmonious architectural space.

Plywood as finish material had been promul-gated by the plywood industry quite early, to judge from industry literature. A pamphlet published in 1937 by the Harbor Plywood Corporation, a manufacturer of Douglas Fir plywood, included commentary by architects as well as builders on the advantages of plywood throughout the build-ing process.[15] Care was taken to represent plywood in both rough and finished construction suitable for all scales of project. Photographs and drawings detail plywood paneling and cabinetry, both painted and natural finish, in domestic settings. One page showing "eight decorative schemes for paneled interiors" includes elaborately dadoed hardwood chair rails and cornices alongside near-flush detailed sliding plywood-door cabinet walls. While eschewing any stylistic affiliations, the eight schemes are all modeled on the familiar idea of crafted wall paneling. Plywood's use as a visible, finish material is thus connoted as rich and luxuri-ous. The line of argument suggested by the images emphasizes for good reason its wood-grained sur-face, not its shear strength, which would also have

Suggested decorating schemes for plywood, Harbor Plywood Corporation

Vertical Plywood sheets with diagonal wainscot

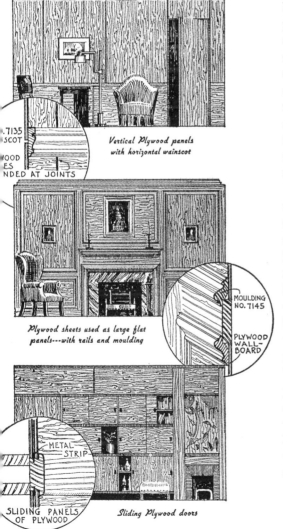

.7135
SCOT

VOOD
ES
NDED AT JOINTS

Vertical Plywood panels with horizontal wainscot

MOULDING
NO. 7145

PLYWOOD
WALL-
BOARD

Plywood sheets used as large flat panels---with rails and moulding

METAL
STRIP

SLIDING PANELS
OF PLYWOOD

Sliding Plywood doors

recommended its use as an excellent wall sheathing: a material associated with rough construction would have no place in the well-appointed drawing rooms shown in the eight images.

The introduction of veneered plywood, especially finer-grained birch and maple which took stains and finishes evenly, unlike the variegated hard and soft grained surface of the Douglas Fir used for the core, allowed much greater control of the material's appearance. This opened the possibility of much more differentiated readings of the plywood surface than simply 'wood-grained'. In discussing his decision-making criteria, Rakatansky describes a near-organic interplay of form, site and occupation as the basis for his work, which he describes as "an enclosure of space around life, for the specific site."[16] His use of plywood also evidences a much more atmospheric spatial sensibility, one in which plywood is connoted not as a particular material or as a cultural statement, but rather an element in the play of enclosing planes.

The Weisberg House of 1949 was one of Rakatansky's most graceful and elegant to date at the time of its construction. Its butterfly roof, open truss carport and didactically cantilevered exterior balcony are all departures from the compact, flat-roofed volume he had used in the Halsband House, built collaboratively with his father in East Greenwich in 1947 and 1948. Although realized, it has been altered significantly and can best be known through drawings. Sited on a sloped plot overlooking the ocean, the sequence through the building begins beneath the carport whose roof structure protrudes from the apparently compact, vertical cedar-sided house. One enters a small wind break, with no indication of the scale of the double-height living room overlooking the ocean. That space, and the Atlantic beyond it, is first seen from the corridor adjoining the windbreak; the entry door is offset

Weisberg House 1949

The Weisberg House was built on Eustis Avenue in Newport, Rhode Island for Mr. and Mrs. William Weisberg and their nine-year-old daughter. Although Mr. Weisberg, a jewelry designer, was from New York, his wife had roots in Newport and the family enjoyed what Rakatansky terms "indoor-outdoor living." The house, placed diagonally on the lot to maximize views to nearby Euclid Beach, is built into the hillside. The street-side entry is single-height but the ocean side, where the ground slopes away, is dominated by a double-height living room. Rakatansky notes that a view

to the Atlantic Ocean was possible on arrival by looking through the window next to the street-side entry to the double height windows in the ocean-side living room, all without invading the residents' privacy.

The Weisberg House, although spare, is complemented by thoughtfully deployed structural elements. For example, the beam that supports the second floor also is a light cove illuminating the living room. As Rakatansky remarks, a ceiling fixture in the double-height space would have meant "calling the fire department to change a bulb." An exposed metal truss that supports

the entrance overhang and part of the carport also provides formal variation to the wood-clad house. The cantilevered balcony on the upper level also makes dramatic use of structure to provide a view of the ocean impeded only by a lacing of bronze rudder cable between broad wooden railings.

from the door to the corridor, obstructing a direct view on entry and heightening the effect of the sequence. An open-tread switch-back stair separates the single-height portions of the house — upstairs bedrooms, downstairs open kitchen and dining area — from the dramatic living room, defined on one side by a huge CMU and brick fireplace wall and perpendicular to it, by enormous fixed plate glass. Birch plywood is specified extensively in this primary space — as door veneer, as finish wall surface, for soffits and fascias, for the sheathing beneath the stair and balcony, and for a small, floating cabinet which the solid maple stair treads penetrate to provide shelves and supporting structure. On the one hand, all these materials underline the house's immediate modernity; none of them, not even the 'common brick', would have been specified as a finish in standard domestic construction of that period or prior. On the other hand, the way in which surfaces are materialized reinforces the architectural readings of scale, space and volume.

Upon descending the first flight of stairs to an intermediary landing, the view into the living room is dominated by the fireplace wall and plate glass windows, the larger pane nearly nine feet wide and twelve feet high, its top aligned with the handrail of the upstairs corridor. The first three feet of the fireplace are common brick, but above that, some fifteen feet high and ten feet in width, is the massive CMU wall which acts as shear wall and chimney. The scale of these elements is commensurate with the ocean view, not with the more delicate dimensions of domestic furnishings. Appropriate in scale to windows and fireplace, the wall surface to the fireplace's left is clad to its full height with birch plywood; the birch-clad door to an adjacent guest room is detailed to sit flush, concealed within the larger surface. The use of

plywood allowed the standard-sized door to be camouflaged, whereas the discrepancy in finish between painted wood and plaster would not have, even if the detailing had been the same. Read as an unbroken plane, this part of the wall maintains its scalar parity to the fireplace and window wall.

On the other side of the room, the birch plywood assumes a different architectural role and scale. The maple stair and birch-clad corridor floor plate (underside, flooring and soffit are all specified in birch plywood) can be read together, much like an element of furniture set into the larger space. As the transition between the house's smaller rooms and its primary space, the stair's transparency and its furniture-like quality allow for the factual subdivision of the spatial volume while allowing the volume to be read, at least implicitly, in its entirety. The floating plywood cabinet, set in alignment with the edge of the fireplace brick, would have reinforced this reading. It also embodies the same slight of hand as the spidery steel web truss, which floats above the carport.

All other vertical surfaces are specified as vermiculite plaster, an iridescent finish which would have broken the reflected light coming off the sand

Weisberg House

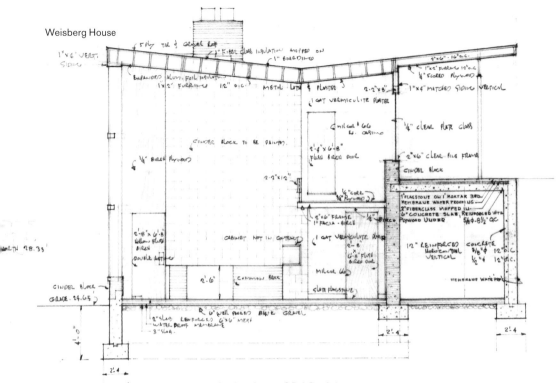

TRANSVERSE SECTION
SCALE 1/4" = 1'-0"

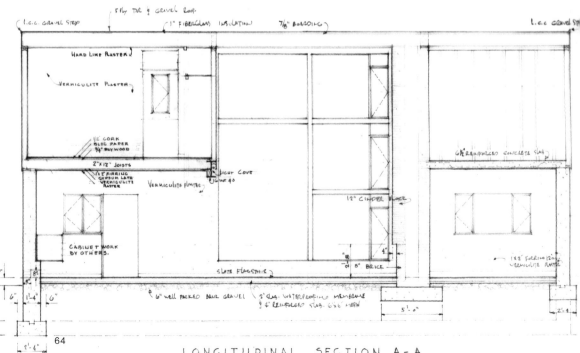

64

LONGITUDINAL SECTION A-A
SCALE 1/4" = 1'-0"

and water. The ceiling was also plastered, but without the vermiculite additive, to create a matte surface. Artificial light was concealed behind soffits in the adjacent single-height dining area and kitchen, but no direct artificial light was specified for the large space. One can imagine the play of light — dappled and vibrant in the daytime, muted and indirect at night — refracting on the vermiculite plaster surfaces, picking up highlights on the yellowish varnished birch, absorbed by the matte CMU and brick surfaces, and flagstone floor. During the day, the horizon was present through the plate glass; at night, the reflections in the glass doubled the interior space's volume.

11 Since 2007, anonymous wood-framed houses dating from the late nineteenth and early twentieth-century have been the subject of field work and study by students at the Rhode Island School of Design Department of Architecture in the construction course Integrated Building Systems I, co-taught by Andrew Tower and LW. Balloon framing with diagonally sheathed wall is a rule almost without exception.

12 Ira Rakatansky recalls clearly his Italian, French-Canadian and Swedish construction crews, and those who worked on his father's sites, as integral to the way wood construction was used in Providence. In conversation with LW, August 17, 2009.

13 The Rhode Island AIA dates the first licensing exam roughly to 1935, not 1945. Rakatansky recalls being the first Jewish architect to pass the licensing exam in the state. According to the Rhode Island state licensing board, NAAB licensing was made standard for the state in 1977. Ira Rakatansky in conversation with LW, October, 2005.

14 Ira Rakatansky, in conversation with LW, August 17, 2009.

15 Harbor Plywood Corporation, *Handbook of Douglas Fir Plywood* (Hoquiam, WA: Harbor Plywood Corp, 1937).

16 Rakatansky in conversation on several occasions, including August 4, 2009.

Weisberg House

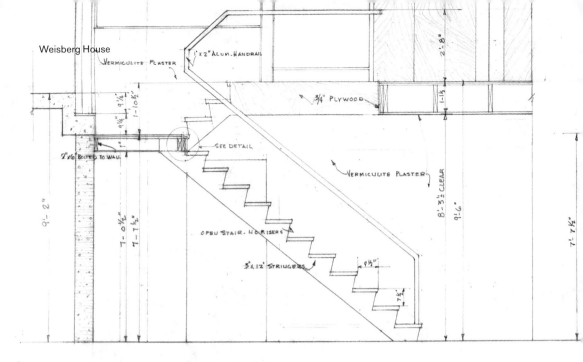

Stair Detail Section labels:

- 1"x2" Alum. Handrail
- Vermiculite Plaster
- 3/4" Plywood
- See Detail
- 2"x6" Bolted to Wall
- Vermiculite Plaster
- Open Stair. 40 Risers
- 3"x12" Stringers
- 2'-8"
- 1-1/4"
- 9 1/4", 1-10 1/2"
- 9'-2"
- 7'-0 1/2", 7'-7 1/2"
- 8'-3 1/2" Clear
- 9'-6"
- 7'-7 1/4"
- 8 1/2"
- 7 1/4"

STAIR DETAIL SECTION
SCALE 1/2" = 1'-0"

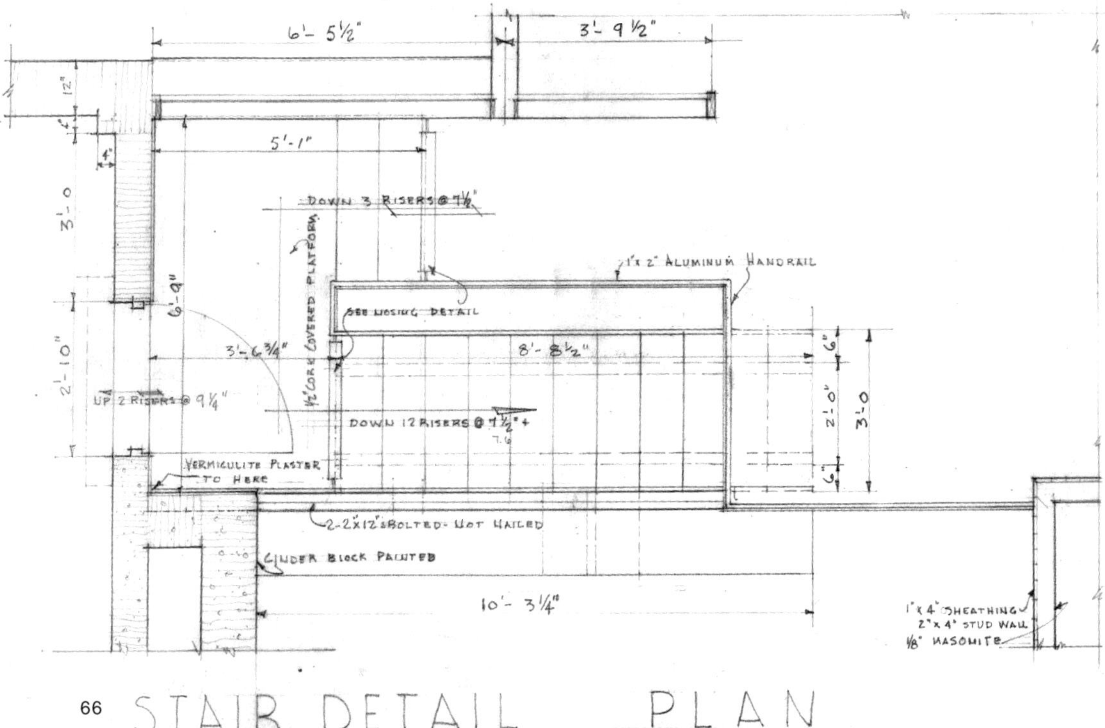

Stair Detail Plan labels:

- 6'-5 1/2"
- 3'-9 1/2"
- 5'-1"
- 12"
- 4"
- 3'-0"
- 6'-9"
- 2'-10"
- Down 3 Risers @ 7 1/2"
- See Nosing Detail
- 1"x2" Aluminum Handrail
- Work Covered Platform
- 8'-8 1/2"
- 3'-6 3/4"
- Up 2 Risers @ 9 1/4"
- Down 12 Risers @ 7 1/2" + 7.6
- Vermiculite Plaster to Here
- 2-2"x12" Bolted - Not Nailed
- Cinder Block Painted
- 10'-3 1/4"
- 6"
- 2'-0", 3'-0"
- 1"x4" Sheathing
- 2"x4" Stud Wall
- 1/8" Masonite

66 ## STAIR DETAIL PLAN
SCALE 1/2" = 1'-0"

HOME SECTION

BUILDING REAL ESTATE HOME DECORATION GARDENING

The Providence Sunday Journal
Section V   August 26, 1951

SUPER-WINDOW and cantilevered balcony at the back look away to the ocean. Window lights living room. Balcony is off master bedroom. The railing is laced with metal rope.

—Staff Photos by H. Raymond Ball

NEW HOME of Mr. and Mrs. William Weisberg on Eustis Avenue, Newport, designed by architect Ira Rakatansky of Providence. One-story high at the street, it drops to gain another story at the rear. Exposed beam supports roof overhang which shelters entrance.

High Style in Newport
Modern Home Sits on Hillside in City of Quaint Dwellings

By DOROTHY AGNEW

NEWPORT, which has complacently looked upon fabulous mansions that classify it as world-famous, and quietly prided itself on some of the oldest buildings on the continent, is now blinking at a dwelling of modern design that has caused a stir in its midst.

It is the new home of Mr. and Mrs. William Weisberg, designed by Ira Rakatansky, Providence architect.

Perched on a hillside off Euclid Avenue, the severely-smart dark-wood, glass and cinder-block struc-

of the room. The front door opens out. The entire shutter may be into a small entry which in turn drawn to one side leaving the window leads into an extensive stair hall. dow free.

Instead of the stairs going up they The stair hall is like a big balcony head down to the main rooms. Two and the living room below can be bedrooms, a bath and linen closets plainly seen over the railing or are on the upper level, two on the down the open stairway.

Each bedroom has a closet wall The living room alone rises the with sliding doors of pale birch. full two stories. The two-story

Each has a specially-designed head-window in the rear wall, which is board for the beds with open 16 feet wide and 22 feet high, lights shelves for books. Above each bed both the living room and the upper

Mr. Weisberg, a jewelry designer, With a railing only on one side, designed a dressing table and had the stairs descend past a white one made up for each bedroom. cinder-block chimney breast and When not in use, it is a table with

just clears the ground and rises almost to the edge of the roof.

Neither the exterior nor the interior employs idle ornamentation. Structural details have been utilized where they might help the design.

Inside, daring colors on patches of plaster wall happily go hand in hand with surfaces of polished natural wood, glass and dead-white cinder blocks.

The outside, more prim, indulges in no eye-catching coloring. Its finish is a combination of cinder blocks painted white, vertical boards with dark brown stain, and glass that catches reflections.

The long low face is divided into two parts. The right half is approximately 10 feet back from the line formed by the left half, and the break in the flat roof continues straight across the face and makes a deep overhang over the setback. The overhang is supported by a slender column at either end. Both the beam and the column are out in the open and treated as decoration.

Surprise in Room Layout

The garage door and the main entrance with its flagstone step are in the shelter of the overhang. The garage blocks. In a corner of cinder blocks faces the street and the front door is in the side at the projecting portion which is faced with wood.

A surprise comes in the layout

shelves beneath it and also within which extends the full depth of the room. There will be room here painted a gray violet, two soft yellow.

Master Bedroom in Rear

The master bedroom is at the rear of the house. A door opens from it to a cantilevered balcony which faces the garden and also marks the beginning of the dining room. The dining end is finished gray with a violet cast. chaise lounge covered in clear yellow and bright red.

The railing for the suspended balcony—which commands a magnificent view—is also a lacing of bronze rubber cable between broad wood rails.

Between the two bedrooms is the spacious bath. It not only has compartments glassed-in for the toilet and seat but also twin lavatories.

Except in the bathroom all flooring on the upper level is cork. The walls in the bedroom-bath area of the hall are paneled in light wood. The remainder of the stretch is plaster painted a vibrant, fresh blue. The wall toward the garage is the red of a red orange. But the blue and blue are separated by a wide window that overlooks the front steps.

No draperies hang at this window. It is equipped with a shutter of vertical slats of stiff white fabric. The slats may be opened or closed to let light in or keep it

with stone which gets polished as regularly as any wood floor. Coils for radiant heat are under the flooring.

The window wall in the living room is on two levels, as is the upper hall. It runs up to a door that opens to the garden and also marks the beginning of the dining room. The dining end is finished gray with a violet cast.

Kitchen on East Side

Location on the street side of the lower level, the kitchen has a breakfast area, furnished like a little dining room in the modern manner, and also a sewing corner. The sewing corner has a built-in cupboard above. Below the counter are drawers and a cupboard in which the portable sewing machine is kept.

Unlike most kitchens, this one has no stove in plain sight. The burners are sunk in the counter. The lightly-polished steel oven door is nearby in a wall panel, placed just the right height to allow Mrs. Weisberg to open it without stooping.

A desk is incorporated in the cabinetwork.

Access to the laundry-storage room beside the kitchen is from the powder room. The powder room has a dressing-table counter on which drops mail deposited in a chute at the front door above.

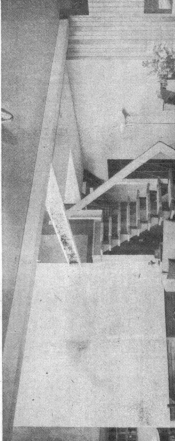

LOOKING DOWN from stair hall to living room and dining room. Entire lower floor is paved with stone. Upper level (shown in upper left corner) is cork.

LIVING ROOM viewed from the dining end. Railing on stairs has same metal lacing as outside balcony. Door showing at head of stairs leads to garage▶

STUDY, secluded behind living-room fireplace, has removable bookshelves resting on brackets.

Reversible Chair 1949

Rakatansky designed the Reversible Chair in the early 1940s, while working in Marcel Breuer's office prior to his graduation from the GSD, in response to a Museum of Modern Art competition for new furniture design. The chair is intended to function as both a lounge and dining chair. By taking both chairs' profiles, then reversing and superimposing them, Rakatansky created a template for his forms: the armrest of the dining chair would, when turned upside down, become the runner for the lounge chair, whose seat was lower to the ground. The chair was supported by a continuous piece of metal to "provide spring action so that the chair would not seem like a rock." He imagined it would be used for dinners at which formal presentations were made. After dinner, the tables would be cleared and the people could flip over the chairs to make themselves more comfortable for presentations.

Unfortunately, the small-scale competition model arrived in pieces, so it was not considered. Nearly ten years later Rakatansky met Frederick Werner, a patent attorney, who arranged for a review of the proposal. Although the patent was initially denied on its first submission in 1949, it was granted in 1952.

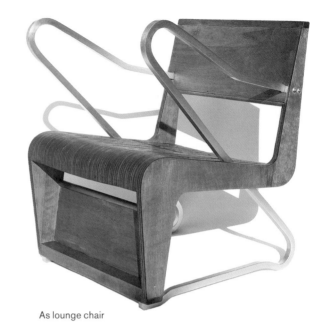

As lounge chair

As dining chair

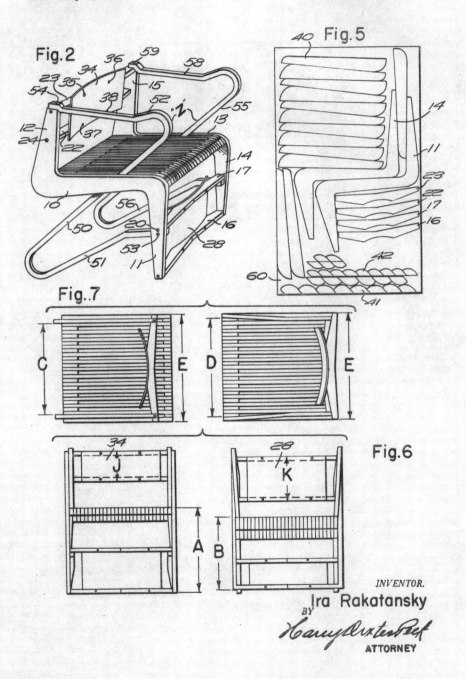

Fig.2

Fig.5

Fig..7

Fig.6

INVENTOR.

Ira Rakatansky

BY

Harry Rixtenbeck

ATTORNEY

Wax House 1950

The Wax House, near Roger Williams Park in Providence, uses a clever layout of space and windows to frame views of the nearby park and create a sense of spaciousness despite its compact 1,700 square foot area—including the garage. With its barely-pitched, deeply overhanging roof and large expanses of glass, it contrasts to the neo-Colonials on both sides.

The way in which Rakatansky still recalls the project's development reflects the extent to which his work was intertwined with the lives of his clients. In this case, Mr. and Mrs. Wax longed to have a child. As Rakatansky recalls, Mrs. Wax became pregnant during the project's development, changing the way in which the house was conceived, for a family rather than for a couple. The Waxes were merchants who had developed a family grocery store into a successful food distribution business.

The Waxes shared the same socio-economic bracket as many of Rakatansky's clients in the 1950s: the new self-made middle class, much like Rakatansky himself. In contrast to members of the older establishment, this new class understood modern architecture as a part of their achievement in forming an identity outside the establishment entrenched in New England. Rakatansky remembers these kinds of clients as "astute observers who wanted something rational, but did not rely on inherited taste," and "brave souls who are intellectual and secure in themselves."

HOME SECTION

The Providence Sunday Journal

BUILDING   REAL ESTATE   HOME DECORATION   GARDENING

Section V.   August 12, 1951

LIVING ROOM has stone floor, is open to the rafters. Chimney breast and supports for seat-and-cabinet unit are cinder blocks. Draperies cover the windows.

GLASS PANELS light up face of new home of Mr. and Mrs. Abraham Wax on Edgewood Boulevard. Left wall and garage, glimpsed beyond corner, are cinder blocks painted white. Front entrance is sheltered by the deep overhang of the roof. Ira Rakatansky was the architect.

Pint-Size Modern

STREET SIDE of living room viewed from dining room. Low doors at the left of the window close off entrance vestibule.

MASTER BEDROOM: Low walls permit a circulation of air from the adjoining rooms. Window in living room is seen above the storage wall which appears as solid wood paneling when doors are closed. Long bank of windows opens up wall facing closets, overlooks garden.

DINING ROOM has no windows of its own. Light comes from living room, also through case in kitchen wall and from bedroom.

Daringly-Different House Blends Cinder Blocks, Glass, Wood

By DOROTHY AGNEW

LAST spring a pint-size house of modern design took shape on a 55x100-foot lot on Edgewood Boulevard. Neighbors looked on in amazement as cinder blocks, great sheets of glass and smooth woods gradually blended into the daringly-different little dwelling.

The owners, Mr. and Mrs. Abraham W. Sarkisian, and the architect, Ira Rakatansky of Providence, unhesitatingly answered questions on the practicability, of heating a house through a stone floor and the effects on comfort of changing outside temperatures on encasing walls of glass.

The one-story structure is larger than it appears at first glance. The interior is amazingly roomy and airy.

Hidden Ell at Back

An ell extending at the back unseen from the street, makes the over-all length greater than the width. Measuring 39 feet across the front, including a garage at the left side, it runs back 44 feet.

Space was left on the small site for a broad lawn at the front and a back yard at the rear of the garage and a back yard of generous proportions. The back yard is secluded by a sapling fence.

The house has five main rooms and a hostler room. Not one is blocked or cramped. A feeling of great spaciousness was achieved by letting the living room and dining room flow into one another as one big area and by keeping some of the partitions from touching the lofty ceiling.

Only the face of the house and the forward half of the right side have big panels of glass opening up the outside walls. Those on the front look toward grassy growth in Roger Williams Park. Those on the side face south over the broad lawn.

A deep overhang of the roof at the front protects windows on that side. Turning the corner, the cinder-block wall runs down the left side of the house to the garage whose face and left side are also in cinder blocks.

In winter the rays of the sun slant in under the roof. In summer they are blocked by the overhang.

A deep overhang of the roof at the front protects windows on that side. Draperies may also be pulled across to close out warming sunshine.

The rooms benefit by solar heat.

and given a high gloss has been used as facing for the rest of the house. It is in sharp contrast to the white wood trim and stretches of white.

On the inside cinder blocks painted white and also in bold vibrant colors vie for attention with areas of richly-toned plaster and wood both natural-finish and painted.

Change of Color Effective

The living room and dining room together make an L-shaped space that turns away from the front and side of the house. The long straight wall toward the garage, belonging partly to the living room, is all cinder blocks. The sudden change of color distinguishes the dining area.

Creamy chocolate, coral and stark white are the colors played up in the living room. The long dining-room is painted coral. The opposite exterior wall of the living room is chocolate color.

The fireplace in the living room has a raised chimney line, of cinder blocks finished white. At the right side of the fireplace a three-

Only the living room lying across the front of the house and the dining room which grows out of it have a stone floor. In summer the stone, heated by water in pipes buried under it, maintains a pleasant consistent warmth.

The bedroom floors are surfaced with cork. Kitchen, the kitchen, back entry and bathroom are finished with asphalt tile.

The interesting, velvety texture of painted cinder blocks has been played up on both the exterior and interior.

An entry protruding at the left end of the face of the house is fronted by a cinder-block panel that reaches from ground to roof line.

Continued on Page Five

—Staff Photos by Edward C. Hassen

Blanding House 1951 Blanding's Pharmacy 1953

Mr. Blanding was, by Rakatansky's account, a distinguished gentleman from a well-established intellectual family and a true patron of the arts. He commissioned Rakatansky to renovate a farmhouse on former agricultural land in Greene, Rhode Island. The existing roof sprang from a four-foot knee wall on the second floor, creating largely unusable space beneath the sloped rafters. In his own words, Rakatansky "opened it up and gave it a soul" by removing one quarter of the second floor area to create a double-height living room overlooked by a second floor balcony. The extensive grounds were designed with landscape architect Ralph Hartman, Mr. Blanding's domestic partner, with whom Rakatansky had collaborated on the Rosen House.

Coincidentally, the Blanding's Pharmacy manager, Sidney Smith, was married to the sister of Rakatansky's dearest friend. This connection and the prior work on his house influenced Blanding to hire Rakatansky to design the new Blanding's Pharmacy in downtown Providence on Westminster Street. This was the more visible of two pharmacies owned by the Blanding family, the other located on Wayland Avenue in a residential area. Rakatansky removed the backs of the window vitrines, so that the store interior was visible from the street.

He designed a large circular soda fountain above which he wanted to hang mobiles by his acquaintance Alexander Calder. Although this proved too expensive, it did result in the one visit Rakatansky made to Calder's workshop. Aluminum panels with light blue baked enamel fronts completed the shop façade.

One read "Ira Rakatansky, designer," as Rakatansky remembers with pride, although he was not yet licensed as an architect.

The pharmacy was destroyed in Hurricane Carol in 1954 and never rebuilt. In a strange anecdote he recalls vividly, Rakatansky, who was in his office at the nearby Arcade Building when the hurricane struck, saw the cases and magazine racks he had designed for the Blanding store washed down Westminster Street by the storm waters.

Pollock House 1953

The Pollock House, designed for a family with three sons, was built on a lot selected in consultation with Rakatansky near Norgate Road in Attleboro, Massachusetts. Ira Pollock was an entrepreneur with a lending agency and Mrs. Pollock was the sister of a local electrician who knew Rakatansky. It was this connection that ultimately led to the commission.

Rakatansky chose a wooded site, on which he oriented the main living spaces to the east and south, away from the access road to the north. Vertical cedar siding was used to make the house blend into its surroundings, which the house in turn engages on the interior through floor to ceiling glass panels in the east and south wall. These large areas of glazing were strategically located in the living and dining rooms which would not need curtains: as Dorothy Agnew of *The Providence Journal* wrote in 1954, "patterns seen through the great windows would be superior to the design on any manmade fabric."

Rakatansky emphasized the free circulation of space on the interior, anchored around a dramatic centrally located fireplace facing the family room, complete with two cylindrical stacks, one for the chimney and one for the furnace. This island also contains an open staircase to the second floor and closed stairs to the basement. A level change of three steps on either side of the fireplace defines the dining room and entryway. Stone pavers on the upper level unified the hall, kitchen and dining room.

Rakatansky remembers fondly receiving the commission. The clients hired him on the spot, paying him two hundred dollars on retainer, at the time his daughter Lynn had just been born. He was delighted to have "a new baby, a new commission and money in my pocket."

Small-scale plans showing arrangement of rooms. First floor is 43 by 31 feet. Second story has a sun deck.

SECOND FLOOR PLAN

FIRST FLOOR PLAN

HOME SECTION

Providence Sunday Journal

BUILDING   REAL ESTATE   HOME DECORATION   GARDENING

Section V.   October 31, 1954

New home of Mr. and Mrs. Ira L. Pollock, Attleboro, designed by Ira Raketansky.

Designed for a Wooded Hill

STORY BY DOROTHY AGNEW — PICTURES BY H. RAYMOND BALL

USUALLY when a client calls in an architect to design a house the building site has been predetermined. But Mr. and Mrs. Ira L. Pollock, had their architect, Ira Rakatansky of Providence, render additional service by choosing the location for their new home. Several sites were under consideration.

The strip of land finally selected was a thickly wooded hillside completely surrounded by trees. The beautiful view would change with the colors of the seasons.

Because of the natural screen provided by the trees, no draperies would be needed in the living room. Also, the patterns seen through the great windows would be so much a part of the design on any man-made fabric.

The house is two stories high but hardly visible from the road-way. The exterior is faced with untouched a half-circle of woods that conceals the face.

Looking north, the face has few windows and none of them on the deliberately played down to enhance the simplicity of the house. A one-story living room wing lying along the left side has a bank of three looking toward the approach. Beyond the end of the wing runs a high wall of cinder blocks painted white and the windows just peek over. In time a cur-

Kitchen extends from the front of the house to dining room at the back. Short work counter and refrigerator back up to low wall guarding the stairway to the basement.

Dramatic-looking island which may be freely circled includes stairways to the second floor and the basement. White stacks are chimneys, one for fireplace, one for heater. Floors in hall, kitchen, dining room are flush and paved with stone.

Dining room is marked off from living room by three steps and change of floor treatment. Door at left opens to porch.

Living room looks away to woods through great panels of glass in east wall. Lower part of window is hinged to open.

Rakatansky House, Lincoln 1954

The Rakatansky House in Lincoln, Rhode Island, was the first home that Rakatansky built for his family. It is located in a wooded area, and was the weekend job site for the architect and the construction crew who worked for his father, a speculative builder. The drawing set reflects the immediacy of this project, reduced as it is to the minimum needed with other information communicated, probably verbally or in sketch form. In 1958, the family moved back to Providence so that the two children could attend public school there.

Though occupied briefly, it is a remarkable home, composed of multiple intersecting planes and spaces that 'continue endlessly', unlike the contained interior of the traditional box shaped New England home. Level change is used adeptly to create privacy while allowing communication amongst all areas of the primary spaces. It clearly illustrates Rakatansky's belief in the primacy of the individual home, always designed to fit within the building site as a particular solution fit to the needs of specific clients.

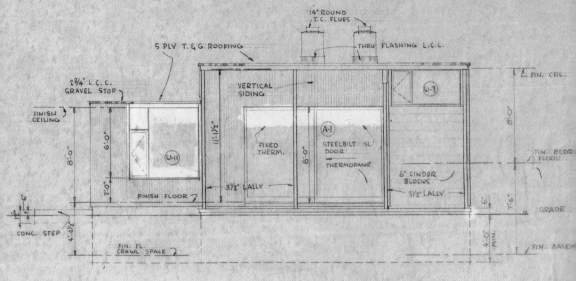

14" ROUND
T.C. FLUES

THRU FLASHING L.C.C.

5 PLY T.&G. ROOFING

2¾" L.C.C.
GRAVEL STOP

VERTICAL
SIDING

FINISH
CEILING

FIN. CEIL.

FIN. BEDR
FLOOR

FIN. BASEM

6'-0"

8'-0"

11'-1½"

8'-0"

8'-0"

7'-6"

W-11

W-7

A-1

FIXED
THERM.

STEELBILT SL.
DOOR

THERMOPANE

6" CINDER
BLOCKS

FINISH FLOOR

3½" LALLY

3½" LALLY

2'-0"

6"

6"

GRADE

6"

1½"

4'-4½"

CONC. STEP

FIN. FL.
CRAWL SPACE

4'-0"
MIN.

EAST ELEVATION

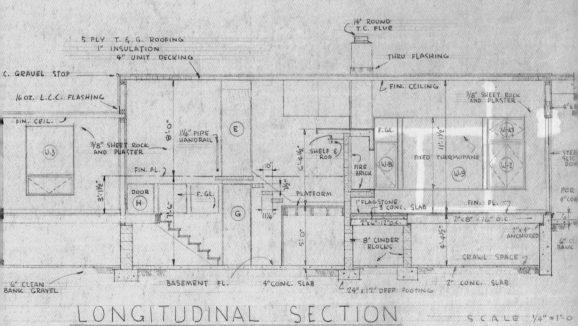

14" ROUND
T.C. FLUE

5 PLY T.&G. ROOFING
1" INSULATION
4" UNIT DECKING

THRU FLASHING

C. GRAVEL STOP

FIN. CEILING

3/8" SHEET ROCK
AND PLASTER

16 OZ. L.C.C. FLASHING

FIN. CEIL.

3/8" SHEET ROCK
AND PLASTER

W-3

FIN. FL.

1¼" PIPE
HANDRAIL

E

8'-0"

F. GL.

W-8

FIXED THERMOPANE

W-1

W-2

SHELF &
ROD

FIRE
BRICK

3'-1½"

DOOR

H

F. GL.

G

1'-6"

10'

1½"

11¼"

PLATFORM

5'-0"

6'-4½"

11'-1½"

1" FLAGSTONE
3" CONC. SLAB

2"x6"-12"O.C.

8" CINDER
BLOCKS

FIN. FL.

2"x8"-16" O.C.

4'-4½"

2"x4"
ANCHORED

CRAWL SPACE

6" CLEAN
BANK GRAVEL

BASEMENT FL.

4" CONC. SLAB

24"x12" DEEP FOOTING

2" CONC. SLAB

LONGITUDINAL SECTION

SCALE ¼" = 1'-0

93

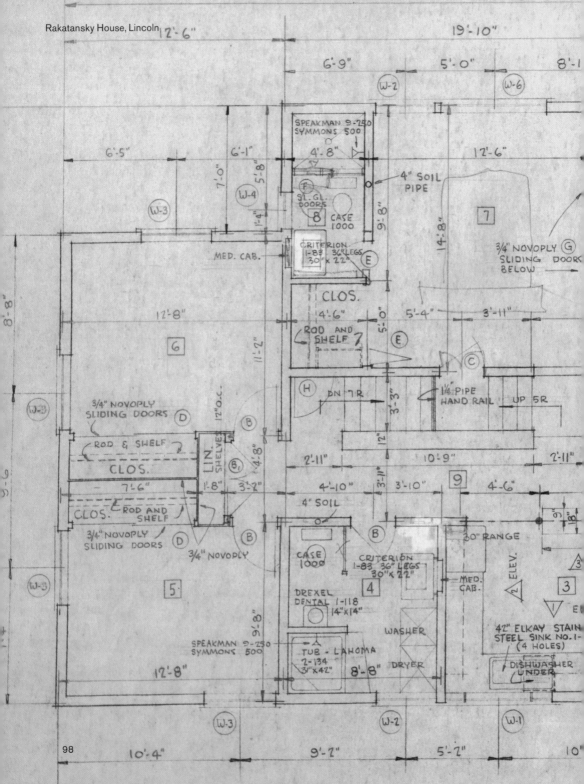

Rakatansky House, Lincoln

98

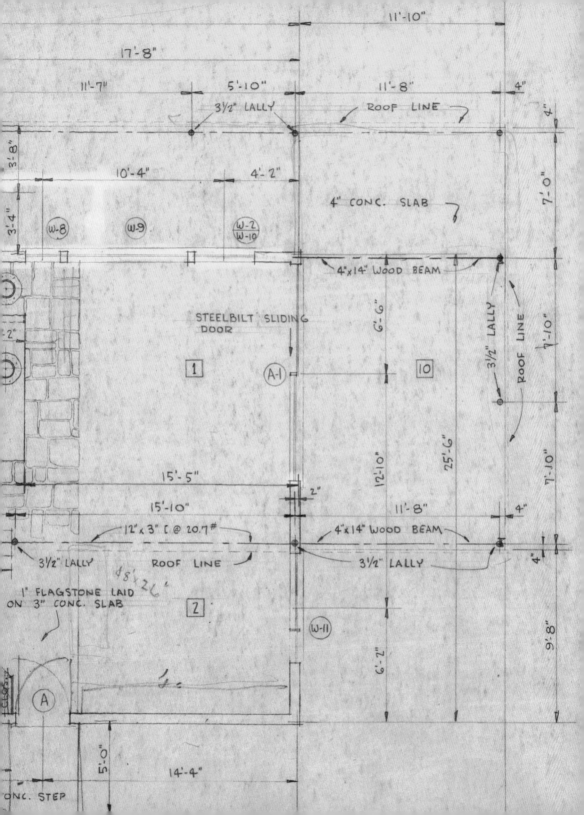

11'-10"

17'-8"

11'-7"   5'-10"   11'-8"   4"

3'-8"   4"

3½" LALLY   ROOF LINE

3'-4"

10'-4"   4'-2"

4" CONC. SLAB

7'-0"

W-8   W-9   W-2 / W-10

4"x14" WOOD BEAM

2"

STEELBILT SLIDING
DOOR

9'-6"

3½" LALLY

ROOF LINE

7'-10"

1   A-1   10

25'-6"

7'-10"

12'-10"

15'-5"

15'-10"   11'-8"   4"

2"

12"x 3" [@ 20.7#   4"x14" WOOD BEAM

4"

3½" LALLY   ROOF LINE   3½" LALLY

48'x 26'

1' FLAGSTONE LAID
ON 3" CONC. SLAB

2

W-11

9'-8"

6'-2"

A

5'-0"

14'-4"

ONC. STEP

HOME SECTION

BUILDING   REAL ESTATE   HOME DECORATION   GARDENING

Providence Sunday Journal   Section V.   January 29, 1956

Street side of house has unassuming entrance approached by wood walk. Facing is narrow hemlock boards laid vertically. Break-through in roof gives high ceiling to living room and space for bedroom on slightly higher level than main floor.

New home of Mr. and Mrs. Ira Rakatansky in Lincoln has wooded setting. Secluded east end has great areas of glass. Roof shelters paved terrace beside living room.

Small-scale plan showing layout of rooms and easy flow of travel from end to end.

An Architect Designs His Own Dream House

...row on the front, door a wide

The land is a wooded acre, with a southwest exposure, on a hillside, along the northerly side of Reservoir Avenue, Lincoln. In the valley below Pawtucket's myriads of lights glimmer at night.

Serenely simple in form and measure in structure blends into the background. The straight sides are faced with narrow, vertical hemlock boarding left to weather. No brilliant accents have been added to catch the eye.

Windows and the front entrance along the street side are unimposing. The end toward the valley is opened up by glass but that is discreetly screened by trees and natural plant growth which were carefully protected during construction.

A low second story noses through the long flat main roof. From the flat roof of the upper

played up into highly dramatic features.

On the main level are several distinct areas. Some flow into one another uninterrupted by partitions. They lend themselves to a low ceiling. The walls find themselves in position if separation of space is desired. Another partition clears both floor and ceiling. Its supports are steel columns that ten and show plainly above and below the partial-height barrier. The only conventional walls are those closing off two bedrooms and a bathroom at the left end of the house.

Living room and dining room share space at that is opened up by glass. The kitchen is at the center front. Running lengthwise back of the kitchen is a passageway extending from the living room to the bedroom area. At the beginning of the pas-

From the front, door a wide brick walk runs straight ahead across the floor to become a hearth in front of the fireplace. The bricks were laid upside down to expose grooves which ordinarily are keys to grip mortar. The grooves make an interesting allover pattern.

The fireplace has a suspended hearth that clears the floor by inches. The floor by is thick and finished on top and sides with small, brown, ceramic tiles. The polished tiles may be easily wiped free of spatter left when steaks or other fatty foods are being cooked over the fire.

Masonry for the fireplace is cinder blocks painted white. Imbedded with the white are various shades at other of the ceiling and out of its top grows a flue encased in a huge white concrete tube. A matching stack rising from the floor at the right end of the fire-

place is the flue for the heating plant in the basement.

White is predominant throughout the interior. Most of the of the woodwork are white. Combined with the white are various shades smooth plaster walls and much ceiling is finished with thick cedar decking, rich dark and highly polished. One wall of the living room and one in the upstairs bedroom are light cocoa

Long view of the interior through sliding glass doors opening to the terrace. In the living room Mr. and Mrs. Raketansky talk with daughter Lynn, 3. Tubular stacks are flues for fireplace and heater. Highly polished ceiling is dark cedar decking. A movable coat closet forms wall at extreme left.

brown. Kitchen floor and counters have pale cocoa-brown toppings.

There are a few accents of sharp light blue. Doors to a linen closet at the bedroom end of the passageway and massive side windows on the upper level and some of the lighting fixtures are blue.

From the upper bedroom every light in the house may be turned

on by means of a series of buttons in the head of the bed. The bed touches no wall and may be freely circled. Its head is a low cabinet with doors opening toward the stairway wall. The electric button panel sunk in the low cabinet on the opposite side are within easy reach without moving head from pillow.

The wall toward the fireplace is half height and the upper part of the living room below is in

view. The wall is a series of closets with sliding doors. They are assigned to Mrs. Raketansky whose dresses, coats, skirts and blouses do not require great height.

Along the opposite wall is a full-height, very deep closet and a small bathroom.

The bathroom on the main floor is large. It has a corner tub raised from the floor and approached by two tile steps. There

is a regulation washbowl, and also a small-size dental bowl for the convenience of daughter Lynn, 3. Space has been given to laundry equipment. Fitted in are automatic washer and dryer. To the left and above is to the bathroom, are two shallow cupboards. One conceals an ironing board hinged to the wall. In the other, nearer the kitchen, are shelves on which canned foods and jellies stand in single lines.

Kitchen has white cabinetwork and light-brown floor covering counter tops. In lower part of open-end wall, right, are compartments for electrical appliances and trays. Shelves pull out of low corner cupboard where Mrs. Raketansky stands.

Low wall at one side of the upper bedroom is closet for apparel that does not require height. A full-height closet and a bathroom open on opposite side of room. Bed may be circled. Head of bed is a low cupboard with opening toward wall.

Rosen House 1955

The Rosen House, built in the Oak Hill neighborhood of Pawtucket, Rhode Island, accommodates the wishes of a conservatively minded family of three within the idiom of High Modernism. Mr. Rosen attended Brown University and ran the family industrial supply business, while Mrs. Rosen came from Central Falls, Rhode Island, and had no previous exposure to contemporary architecture and tended to traditional taste. The family decided to settle in Pawtucket, where they had extended family. They bought a small lot on an embankment, about 75 by 75 feet. Rakatansky's solution to the problem of the small lot and the traditional appearance of the neighborhood was ingenious. The home has a pitched roof, which provides the living room with one-and-a-half floor-height ceilings. It also allows the house to fit in with the contextual neo-Tudors and neo-Colonials of the neighborhood.

Rakatansky also provided a skillful resolution to accommodating the automobile. The driveway runs a short distance from the street down to a garage underneath the master bedroom at the front of the house, and is on grade with the street. This sectional solution maximized the open space around the house, and was particular to the site's topography. Attention to these particularities is central to Rakatansky's design philosophy: he compares a formulaic approach to house design despite siting and client difference to a lifestyle in which "…every meal is the same, boiled chicken and cold potatoes, only the plate is turned."

Living room has two parts. The space at right of the fireplace is a library with dark wood ceiling.

HOME SECTION

Classified Advertising

Providence Sunday Journal

May 4, 1958

Spacious Home Utilizes Small Lot

STORY BY DOROTHY AGNEW

PHOTOS BY H. RAYMOND BALL

"WHAT KIND of a house can five-room house with integral garage. With discretion, the windows in the near-by houses were of fine quality. Mr. and Mrs. Rosen and their architect, Ira Rakatansky, realized its possibilities. The strip has lent itself to a

niture. The living room has a stationary desk-bookcase unit. Panels of trays and drawers are part of the equipment of the bedroom closets.

cious interior. Rooms, all with white walls except for a few well-placed touches of color, are opened up by big areas of glass.

Kitchen has laundry area which Mrs. Rosen closes off with folding shutter-doors.

One bedroom is on higher level than other rooms. The garage is beneath this room.

Den may be converted into bedroom. Niche with TV and record player is a closet.

Home of Mr. and Mrs. Herbert L. Rosen was designed to fit a small lot in well built-up neighborhood. Exterior is all white.

Franek House and Office 1955

The Franek House was built for the family of Dr. Bruno Franek in East Greenwich, Rhode Island. The German-born Franeks had purchased a sloped corner lot on Division Street, near the Warwick and East Greenwich line, to build their home and the site of Dr. Franek's medical practice. Rakatansky's design provided two separate street addresses.

Dr. Franek's psychiatric patients were assured privacy, since they were able to walk directly into the lower-level office from Division Street without encountering the doctor's family. The entrance to the family home, located on the second floor of the building, faced the side street. The sloped terrain allowed street-level access to both house and office.

Unlike many of Rakatansky's clients, the Franeks had been exposed to modern architecture in Germany before the World War II. Because of this, they requested a living room with a high ceiling and narrow, vertically oriented casement windows that required hardware ordered from Germany. Rakatansky was only too happy to oblige his clients, particularly since he found casement windows far more logical than traditional double hung windows. In contrast to the double hung windows, which can only open fifty percent of the overall aperture, casement windows "catch the air like a sail."

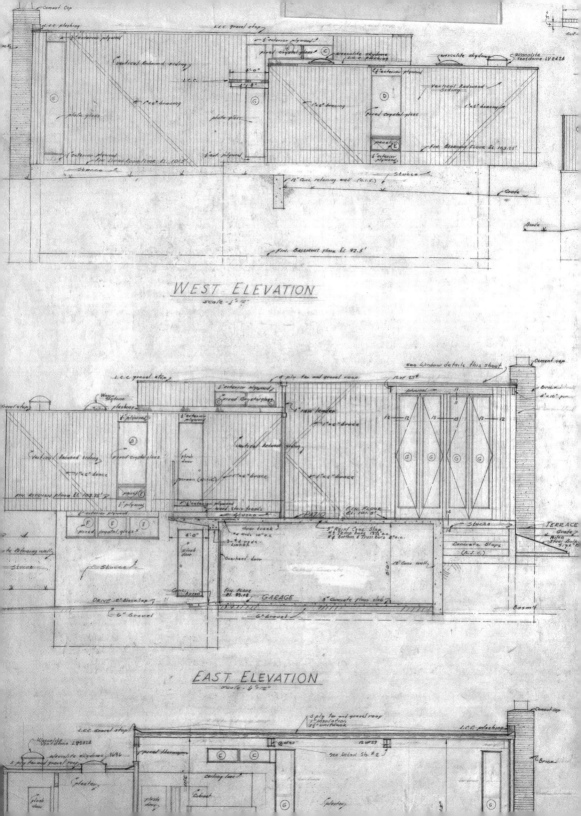

WEST ELEVATION
scale ⅛" = 1'

EAST ELEVATION
scale ⅛" = 1'

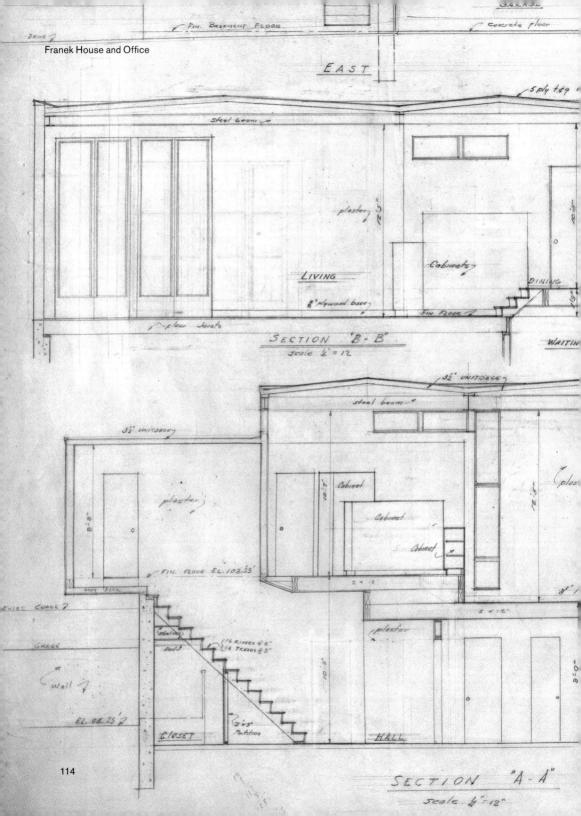

Franek House and Office

114

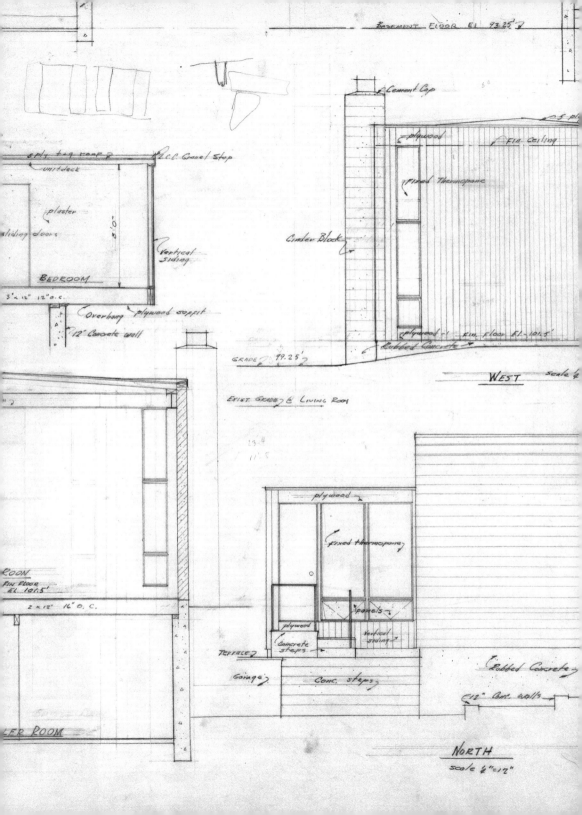

BASEMENT FLOOR EL 93.25' ⊥

Cement Cap

5 pl

plywood   Fin. Ceiling

Fixed Thermopane

Cinder Block

sply tag roof ⊥
unit deck   P.C.C. Gravel Stop

plaster

sliding doors   8'-0"

Vertical
siding

BEDROOM

3" x 12" 12" o.c.

Overhang   plywood soffit

12" Concrete wall

plywood   Fin. Floor El. 101.5'

Rubbed Concrete

GRADE   99.25' ⊥

WEST   scale ¼

EXIST. GRADE @ LIVING ROOM

23.4
11.5

plywood

Fixed thermopane

ROOM

Fin. Floor
EL. 101.5'

panels

2 x 12" 16" O.C.

plywood

Vertical
siding

Rubbed Concrete

Terrace

Concrete
steps

Garage   Conc. steps.

12" Conc. walls

ER ROOM

NORTH
scale ¼"=1'2"

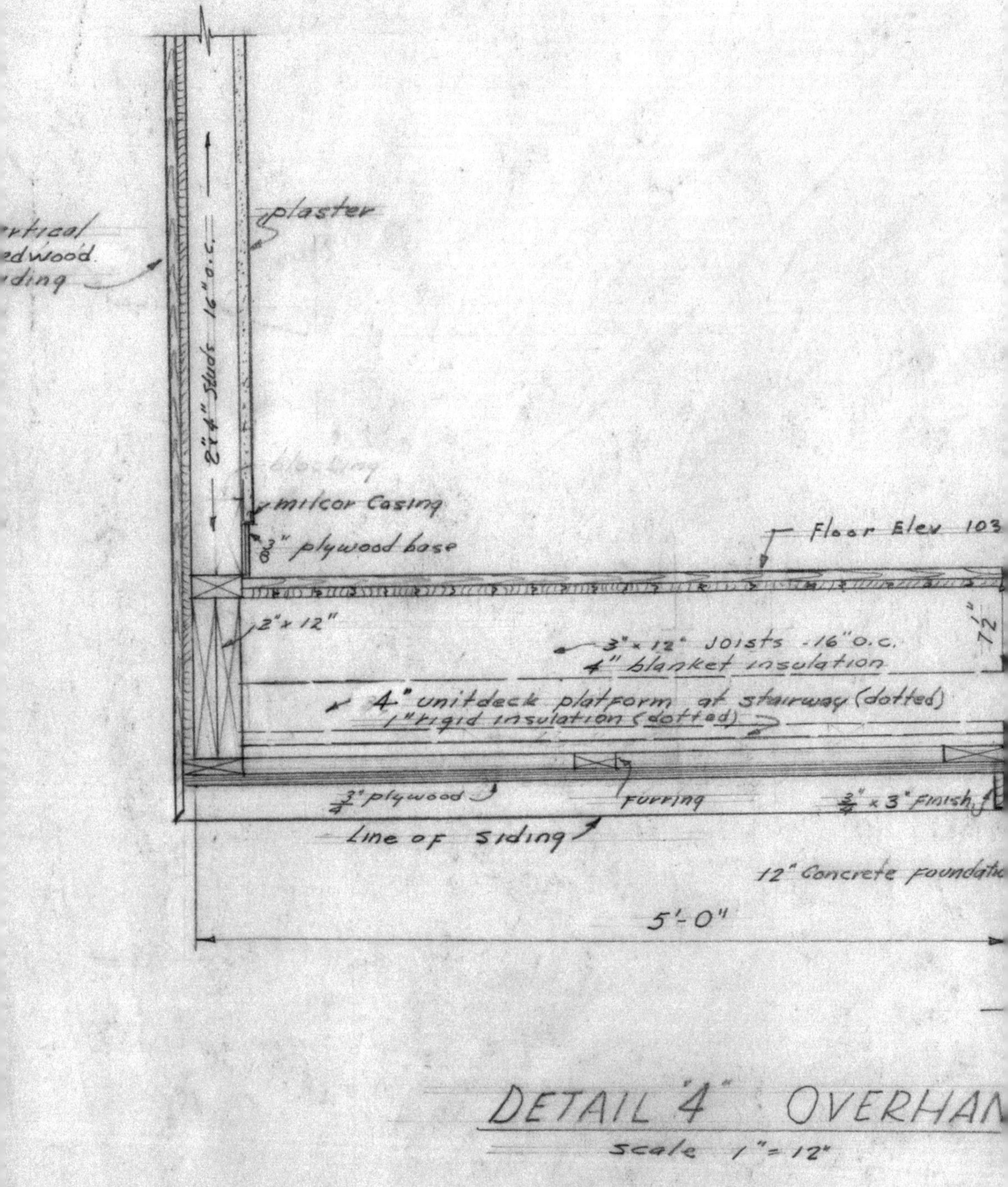

plaster

vertical
redwood
siding

2"x4" Studs 16" o.c.

blocking
milcor Casing
3/8" plywood base

Floor Elev 103

2"x 12"

3"x 12" JOISTS -16" o.c.
4" blanket insulation

4" unitdeck platform at stairway (dotted)
1" rigid insulation (dotted)

3/8" plywood
furring
3/4"x 3" finish

line of siding

12" Concrete foundation

7½"

5'-0"

DETAIL "4" OVERHAN

scale 1"=12"

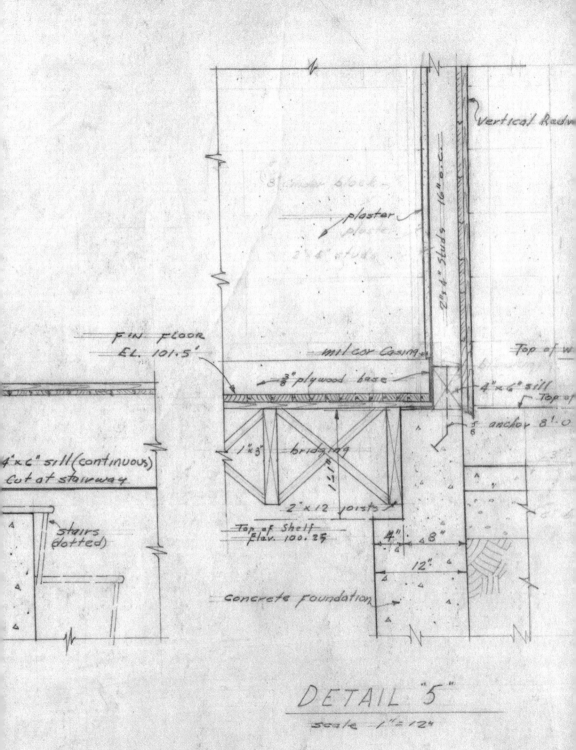

Vertical Radw

8" cinder block

plaster

2" x 4" studs

2" x 4" Studs — 16" o.c.

FIN FLOOR
EL. 101.5'

int'or Casing

Top of w

$\frac{3}{8}$" plywood base

4" x 6" sill

Top of

1" x 3"   bridging

$\frac{5}{8}$ anchor 8'-0

4" x 6" sill (continuous)
cut at stairway

2" x 12 joists

stairs
(dotted)

Top of Shelf
Elev. 100.25

4"   8"

12"

concrete foundation

DETAIL "5"

scale 1" = 12"

Neighbors Look Twice

Controversial dwelling in old East Greenwich is new home of Dr. and Mrs. Bruno Franek. Flat roof is hidden.

house is surrounded by traditional houses, some of which are held in high esteem by antiquarians.

Reactionaries in town looked on with apprehension as the new structure took shape. The modern-minded openly expressed approval. Comments are now freely being voiced, for and against.

The owners had sound reasoning in back of the decision to build a house of contemporary design. Both had a hunger for light, airy, spacious rooms. Although they met for the first time in America and married here, their backgrounds were foreign and similar. Each lived in Germany until the end of World War II. Their homes gone, each experienced cramped quarters.

Eager to speak of their new home, planted so solidly on the steep slope, Mrs. Franek enthused: "From the streets it might look a little severe and not too inviting. But, oh, the inside it opens up so wide and high."

Along Division Street hill the house is two stories high

glass on the two long sides give generous glimpses of the trees in the yard and a view of Narragansett Bay at the east.

The glass panels on the side towards the water are 12-foot-high doors that open to a sun deck atop the garage. The garage is approached from the lower level on Division Street.

Walls of the room are stark white. The ceiling is of natural wood with structural steel beams deliberately left exposed as part of the decorative pattern.

The two short ends of the room have special interest. The north end, without windows, is dominated by a tremendous mosaic mural worked in place by the doctor and Mrs. Franek. The mural contains thousands of small pieces of Venetian glass patiently cut to size and placed to build up into a pattern.

At the south side of the living room three steps lead up to a dining room.

STORY BY DOROTHY AGNEW—PICTURES BY THOMAS D. STEVENS

Looking down on living room from elevated dining room. Owners made the impressive, richly colored mosaic mural.

Family group in the wide, high-ceiling living room: Both Dr. and Mrs. Franek are musicians and there is plenty of floor space for the grand piano. Tall panels of glass, at right, are doors opening onto a patio on garage roof.

Dining room, where Mrs. Franek stands, is raised above the living room. Small entrance hall is at right of steps.

Miller House 1956

The Miller House was built for a successful couple from Chicago who had already owned three homes 'enhanced by Rakatansky.' The Lloyd Avenue house was also a conversion from a large barn to a home. The barn was set back on the lot, affording quiet and privacy from the street. As the structure was rather close to the property line, Rakatansky and the Millers were required to go to the local zoning board to receive a variance on the rear yard, in order to turn the barn into a permanent residence.

In transforming the barn, Rakatansky removed the hayloft, turning the building into a single story structure. As a nod to the house's origins, he playfully kept a wooden truss from the barn, waterproofed it, and left it visible from the exterior of the building. Rakatansky recalls the clients' home as a 'joyful' one bedroom, anchored by a central fireplace and lit up by colorful Ecuadorian fabrics that Mr. Miller had purchased while procuring lumber for the war effort ten years before.

Myers House and Office 1958

The Myers House was built near Wayland Square in Providence for Dr. Myers and his wife. The doctor was a psychiatrist and a former German refugee who had escaped the National Socialists by emigrating to China before World War II. As psychiatry was stigmatized in the 1950s, Rakatansky positioned the office on the ground floor, which disguised the office behind a domestic façade.

The apartment that the doctor shared with his wife was located on a single level above the office.

There is a remarkable amount of storage, and the storage elements subdivide the space into different zones around a central core that contains the skylit kitchen.

The house is faced with vertical wooden siding. Rakatansky believes that wood sheathing must be positioned vertically, and that horizontal sheathing is the reason for rot, particularly in gutters and sills.

Rakatansky devised a sectional solution to the problem of privacy for the doctor's patients. Patients entered the building by descend-

ing a couple of stairs to the waiting room. The receptionist admitted patients to the consultation space behind. After the patient had seen the doctor, he could exit through a second door to the stair landing adjoining the main entrance, thus bypassing the waiting room.

This circulation space was also useful for the doctor, as it enabled him to traverse the distance between his second floor apartment and the office below without exiting the building.

Blieden House 1958

The Blieden House is located in Warwick, Rhode Island, within Governor Francis Farms post-war housing development. Although the 2,000-square-foot house sits comfortably on a large 184,000-square-foot corner lot, Rakatansky struggled with the problem of how to build a modern home in a neighborhood largely consisting of "Queen Anne fronts and Mary Jane behinds." Rakatansky's solution was an 'inside out colonial', in which the house's more solid back, complete with pitched roof, faces the streets and the largely glass front of the house is oriented to the interior of the lot.

Like many of Rakatansky's houses, the sense of space in the interior is a surprise to the visitor upon entry. Not tied to the belief that a house's exterior must be the imprint of its interior, Rakatansky has said instead that to "honor the house, know the space." The home is laid out into two parts, the living areas and the bedroom areas, divided by a diamond-shaped fireplace near the main entrance. The living areas are positioned to the west and the bedroom areas lay to the east, in order to catch the morning sun. In addition, Rakatansky provided ample space for the two sons, aged six and eight, to play. The house itself was a substantial expense for the young family, and Rakatansky fully understood that budget required the Bliedens to retain some of their older furniture.

This attitude is a hallmark of Rakatansky's dealing with clients, who he knew were not quite ready to "thumb their nose at society, but knew it wasn't for them."

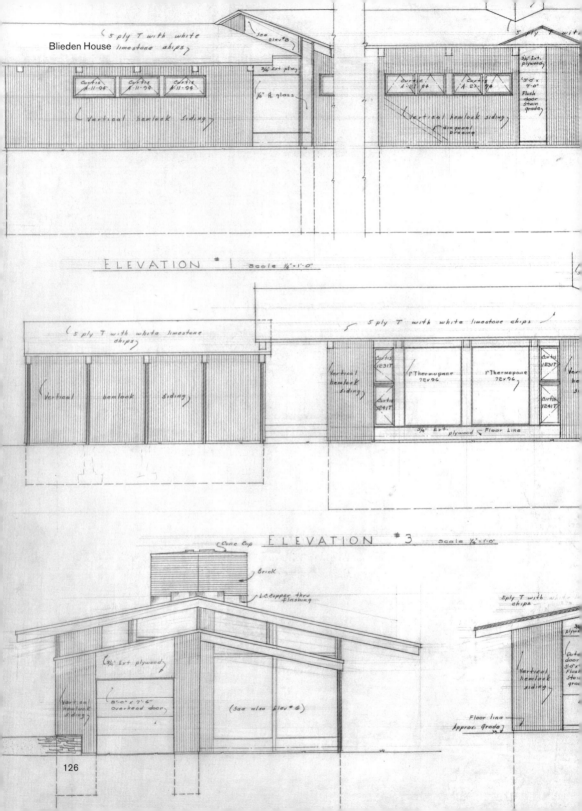

Blieden House

(5 ply T with white limestone chips)

Curtis A-11-94 Curtis A-11-94 Curtis A-11-94

See Elev #B

3/4" Ext ply.

1/6" R. glass

(Vertical hemlock siding)

5 ply T with white

3/4" Ext. plywood

Curtis A-21-94 Curtis A-21-94

3'-0" x 7'-0" Flush door Stain grade

(Vertical hemlock siding)

diagonal bracing

ELEVATION #1   Scale 1/4"=1'-0"

(5 ply T with white limestone chips)

5 ply T with white limestone chips

(Vertical hemlock siding)

(Vertical hemlock siding)

Curtis 1231T

Curtis 1241T

1" Thermopane 72x96

1" Thermopane 72x96

Curtis 1231T

Curtis 1241T

Ver he s

3/4" Ext. plywood   Floor Line

ELEVATION #3   Scale 1/4"=1'-0"

Cone cap

Brick

1.C copper thru flashing

5ply T with white chips

3/4" Ext plywood

(3/4" Ext plywood)

Date door 3'-0" Stain grac

Vertical hemlock siding

Vertical hemlock siding

8'-0" x 7'-6" overhead door

(See also Elev #6)

Floor line Approx. grade

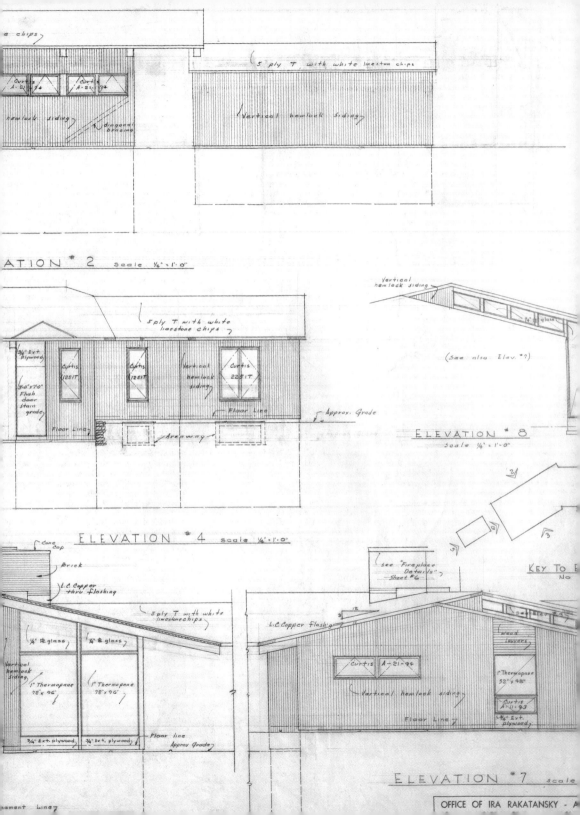

e chips

5 ply T. with white limeston chips

Curtis
A-21-94   Curtis
A-21-94

hemlock siding   diagonal bracing

Vertical hemlock siding

ATION #2   scale ¼" = 1'.0"

Vertical hemlock siding

¼" pl glass

(See also Elev. #7)

ELEVATION #8
scale ¼" = 1'.0"

5 ply T. with white limestone chips

¾" Ext.
plywood

Curtis
1251T   Curtis
1251T   Vertical
hemlock
siding   Curtis
2251T

3'.0"x7'.0"
Flush
door
stain
grade

Floor Line   Floor Line   Areaway   Approx. Grade

ELEVATION #4   scale ¼" = 1'.0"

Cere
Cap
Brick
L.C. Copper
thru Flashing

5 ply T. with white
limestonechips

see "Fireplace
Details"
Sheet #6

KEY TO E
No

¼" pl glass   ¼" pl glass   L.C.Copper Flashing

wood
louvers

Vertical
hemlock
siding

Curtis A-21-94

1" Thermopane
52"x48"

1" Thermopane
78"x96"   1" Thermopane
78"x96"   Vertical hemlock siding

Curtis
A-11-93

¾" Ext.
plywood

¾" Ext. plywood   ¾" Ext. plywood   Floor line
Approx Grade   Floor Line   ¾" Ext.
plywood

sement Line

ELEVATION #7   scale

OFFICE OF IRA RAKATANSKY - A

Blieden House

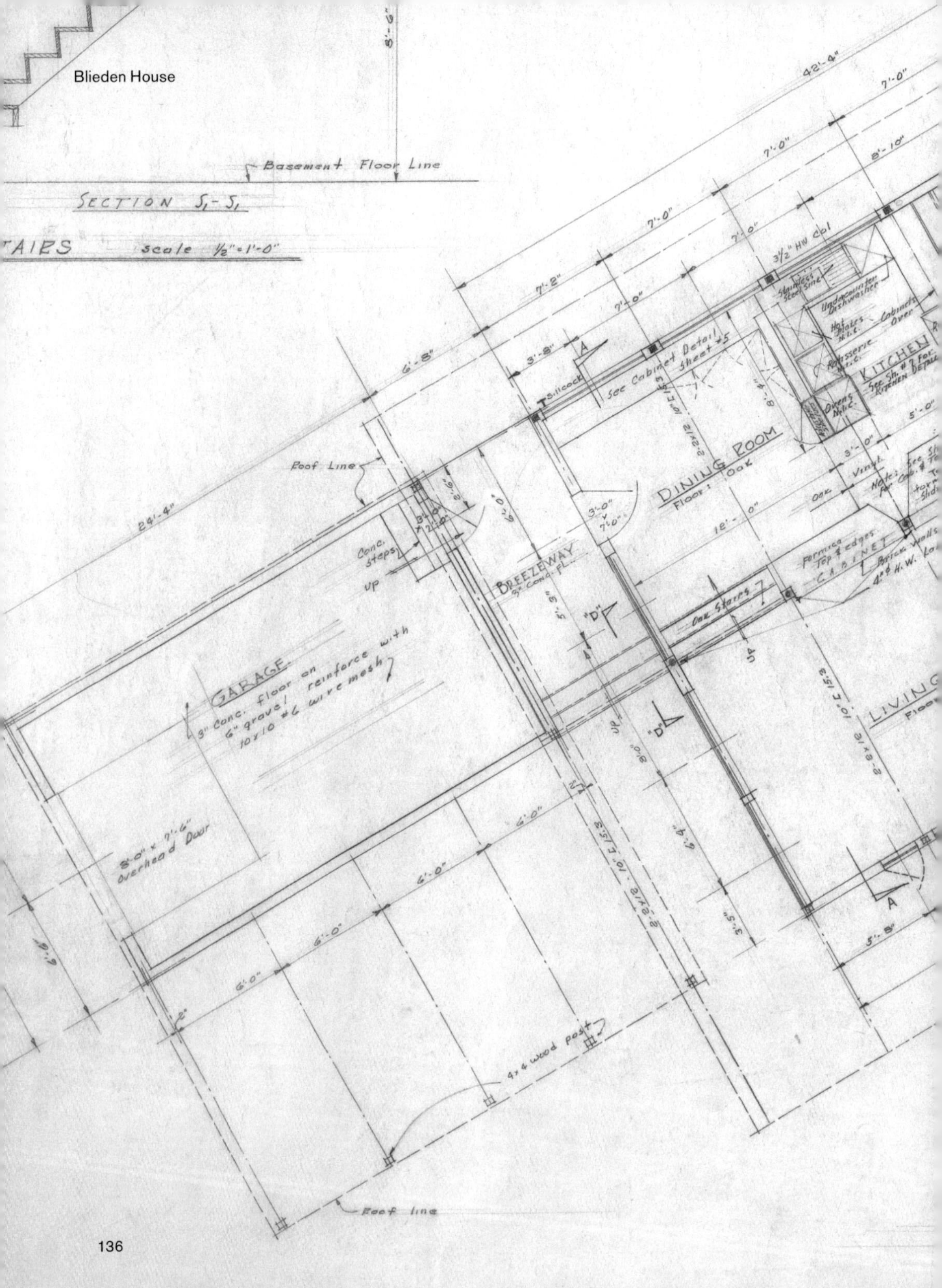

← Basement Floor Line

SECTION S_1-S_1

TAIRS   scale ½"=1'-0"

Roof Line

24'-4"

6'-8"

GARAGE
3" conc. floor on
6" gravel reinforce with
10×10 #6 wire mesh

8'-0" × 7'-6"
overhead Door

6'-0"

6'-0"

Roof line

4×4 wood post

42'-4"

7'-0"

7'-0"

8'-10"

7'-0"

7'-2"

3'-8"   A

Sillcock

3½" HW cpl

Undercounter
Dishwasher

Heater
N.I.C.
Cabinets
Over

Rotisserie
N.I.C.

Owens
Mfd

KITCHEN
See Sh. # for
Kitchen Detail

See Cabinet Detail S
sheet S

5'-0"

DINING ROOM
Floor: Oak

3'-0"

Vinyl

Note: See Sh.
for toy Tos
Slider

18'-0"

5'-0"
×
7'-0"

Conc.
steps
UP

BREEZEWAY
3" Conc. Fl.

5'-3"

"D"

Oak Stairs

Formed
Top & edges
CABINET

Brick walls
4" H.W. L.

LIVING R
Floor

3'-5"

4'-9"

3'-5"

5'-8"

A

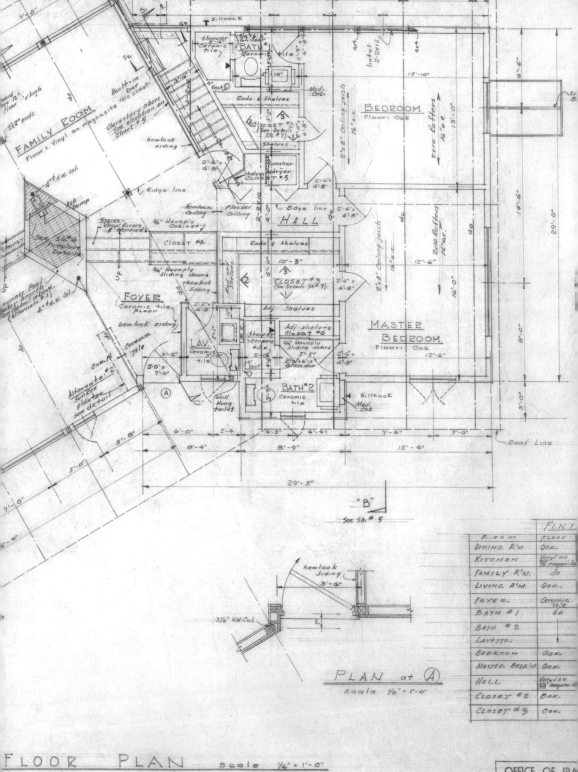

FLOOR PLAN   scale ¼"=1'-0"

PLAN at Ⓐ
scale ⅛"=1'-0"

FAMILY ROOM
Floor: Vinyl on magnasite

FOYER
Ceramic tile floor

LAV.
Ceramic tile

BATH #2
Ceramic tile

HALL

BATH
Ceramic tile

BEDROOM
Floor: Oak

MASTER BEDROOM
Floor: Oak

Closet #4

CLOSET #5

CLOSET #3
(See Details Sh. 7)

"B"
See Sh. # 5

ROOM	FLOOR
DINING R'M	OAK
KITCHEN	Vinyl on ⅝ magnasite
FAMILY R'M.	do
LIVING R'M	OAK
FOYER	Ceramic Tile
BATH #1	do
BATH #2	
LAVETTE	
BEDROOM	OAK
MASTER BEDR'M	OAK
HALL	Vinyl on ⅝ magnasite
CLOSET #2	OAK
CLOSET #3	OAK

OFFICE OF IRA
ROOM 48 ARCADE

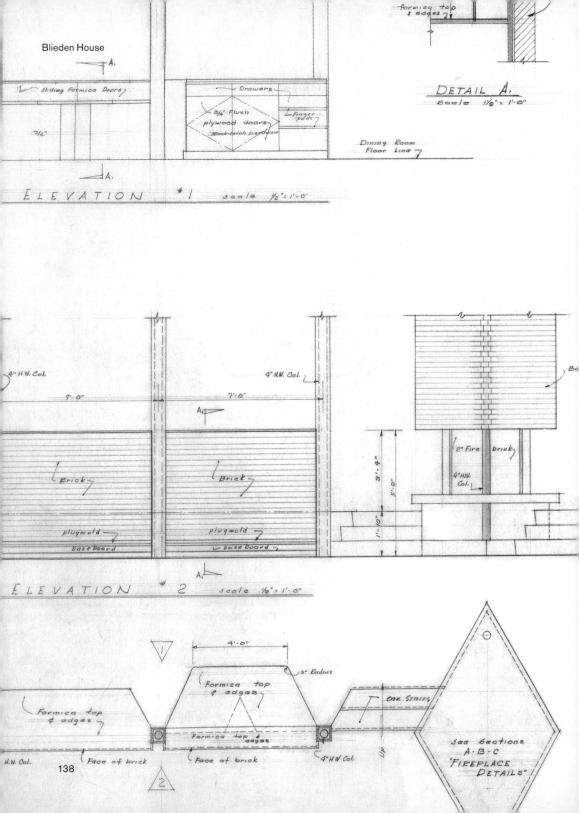

Blieden House

Sliding Formica Doors

3/4"

Drawers

3/4" Flush
plywood doors
touch-latch hardware

Finger
pulls

forming top
& edges

DETAIL A₁
scale 1½" = 1'-0"

Dining Room
Floor Line

ELEVATION #1   scale ½"=1'-0"

4" H.W. Col.

7'-0"

4" H.W. Col.

7'-0"

A₁

B

2" Fire brick

4" H.W.
Col.

Brick

Brick

3'-4"

5'-0"

plugmold

plugmold

baseboard

baseboard

1'-0"

A₁

ELEVATION #2   scale ½"=1'-0"

4'-0"

3" Radius

Formica top
& edges

Oak Stairs

Formica top
& edges

Formica top
& edges

UP

See Sections
A·B·C
"FIREPLACE
DETAILS"

H.W. Col.

Face of brick

Face of brick

4" H.W. Col.

138

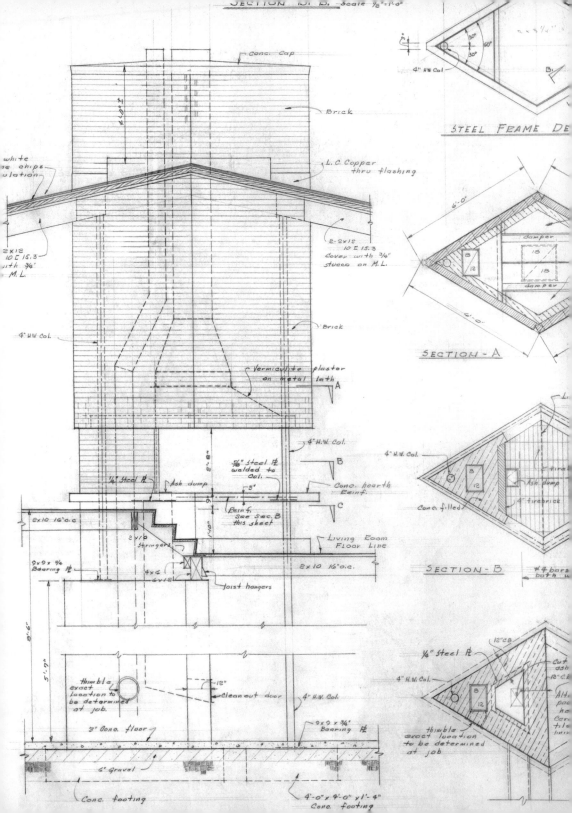

SECTION 151 B. Scale ⅛"=1'-0"

Conc. Cap

Brick

L. C. Copper thru flashing

white
ne chips
ulation

2x12
10 [15.3
ith ¾"
M.L.

2-2x12
10 [15.3
Cover with ¾"
stucco on M.L.

4" HW Col.

Brick

Vermiculite plaster
on metal lath

A

⅝" steel ℔
welded to
Col.

4" H.W. Col.

2'-8"

¼" Steel ℔

Ash dump

5"

Reinf.
See Sec. B
this sheet

Conc. hearth
Reinf.

B

C

2x10 16"o.c.

2x12
Stringers

9x9x¾
Bearing ℔

4x6
6x12

9"

1'-0"

Joist hangers

Living Room
Floor Line

2x10 16"o.c.

8'-6"

5'-9"

Thimble
exact
location to
be determined
at job.

3" Conc. floor

12"

Cleanout door

4" H.W. Col.

9x9x¾"
Bearing ℔

6" Gravel

Conc. footing

4'-0"x 4'-0" y 1'-4"
Conc. footing

STEEL FRAME DE

4" HW Col.

30°
60°
30°

B

6'-0"

5'-0"

damper

18

8
12

18

damper

SECTION-A

4" H.W. Col.

8
12

Ash dump

firebrick

4" firebrick

Conc. filled

SECTION-B

#4 bars
both u

12"C.B.

¼" Steel ℔

Cut
ash
12" C.B.

4" H.W. Col.

8
12

thimble
exact location
to be determined
at job

Kitchen is raised above the living room. Below is shown the sweep through kitchen and dining room.

Looming up with great dignity the big, white triangular-shape fireplace is an impressive interior feature in the new home of Mr. and Mrs. Milton Bleiden, Warwick.

TURNING its back on a street is something a house is not expected to do. But the new home of Mr. and Mrs. Milton Bleiden does just that.

Located on a corner lot it stands with its back to Wauregan Drive and one short end to Nashuena Drive in the Governor Francis Farms section of Warwick. Far in from the side street, facing a secluded garden, is the living area which gives pleasant privacy to the family of four.

The house, planned by architect Ira Rakatansky, is of contemporary design. Walls facing the garden are opened by great windows that seem to make outdoors part of the rooms fortunate enough to enjoy that view. Windows on the street side are more modest in size and the solid wall spaces more extensive.

Exterior finish of the long one-story house is natural-tone hemlock with white trim. There is a deep overhang and in that overhang exposed wood-and-steel beams encased in white stucco show boldly. The roof is topped with white marble chips.

Inside a long living room is open to the white

rafters. And from this spacious room steps go up near each of the two opposite ends to a dining room and kitchen which look over the living room to the outdoors. Also on the upper level are a family room which is in itself walled off and the bedroom area which is a unit in itself.

Dominating the living area is a huge triangular-shape chimney of brick painted white that rises dramatically beside one of the flights of steps to the upper level. In the chimney there is a fireplace with a triangular floor. Beneath the firebox, near the level of the living room floor, is a triangular shape pool.

The garden to which the main rooms look was designed by Robert Hartman, landscape architect, to require a minimum of maintenance. Planting is confined to small well-placed raised beds edged by railroad ties. A big area just outside the big windows is sprinkled with gravel and centered by a weathered wood figure.

On the street side there is just plain smooth lawn. That does not take care but it is cool and green.

Exterior of the house has beautiful play of light and shade due to the boldness of the structural elements.

Secluded garden is the view through the wide windows of the living room. The main entrance is at the left.

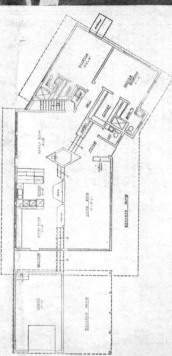

Plan showing house curving slightly away from streets, Wauregan Drive at the back, Nashuena Drive at left.

Rakatansky House, Providence 1958

Rakatansky's current home, located on Everett Avenue in Providence, is a strong expression of his views on the purpose of architecture. In contrast to traditional homes, which Rakatansky feels are not relevant to the way modern families live – "they are dry and one can heat them, but that is about it" – the design of his home considers the orientation of the sun, wind, accessibility, views and utilities.

The existing red-brick carriage house was the starting point of the design. The modern addition surrounds the carriage house on the front and western sides of the house. The brick is painted white on the inside, but Rakatansky left it red on the outside so it would still match its former main house.

Although notable for its relationship to the surrounding landscape, which both hides the home from the street and provides framed views of local foliage, Rakatansky holds landscape architecture as secondary to the construction of architecture. A building should conform to the site, but should not have to twist around man-made landscaping. The landscape architect should aid and assist the work of an architect, who also must know how to design the land, in order to place the building successfully.

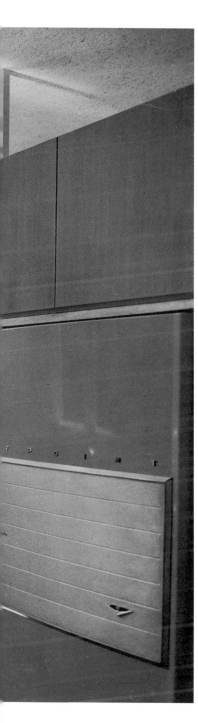

153

15 Meeting Street 1959, 1981

Rakatansky's first office was in the Providence Arcade, a neoclassical 1840s landmark connecting busy Westminster and Weybosset Streets downtown. However, in the early 1950s, when the family moved from Lincoln, Rhode Island to their new home on Everett Avenue, Rakatansky realized that, for his office, too, he wanted to design a space himself and no longer wanted to be a tenant.

Rakatansky found a single-story garage at 15 Meeting Street that covered the entire lot to the street edge. Consistent with his approach to other renovations, his reconfiguration was radical, eliminating half of the existing structure. Nonetheless, he reused much of the old material: old planking was used for the subfloor, and the foundations of the front wall were left standing to enclose the parking lot in front of the office.

Rakatansky's decision to set back the structure to allow for street-front client parking required special permission from the building board of review. As a result, all lot line clerestory windows also had to be glazed with wire glass.

As many as twelve worked in the office at one time, though generally his employees numbered four to five, to which the space was ideally suited. Clerestory windows reveal the sky and trees; they also shield neighboring buildings from view and provide for privacy.

Currently, a visitor would find Lenore Gray sitting just the front door, with her gallery occupying the main room and the one to the right. Rakatansky's office is to the left of the main room with workspace to the rear. Both Rakatansky and Gray sit at large marble and steel tables designed by Rakatansky. A financial firm has rented the upstairs since that level was added in 1981.

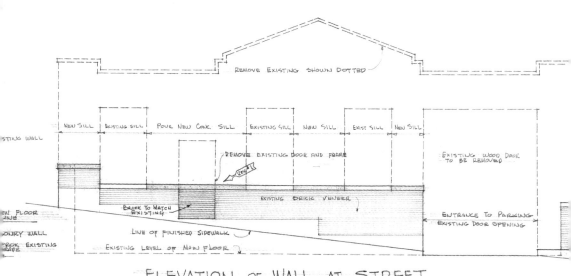

REMOVE EXISTING SHOWN DOTTED

NEW SILL | EXISTING SILL | POUR NEW CONC. SILL | EXISTING SILL | NEW SILL | EXIST SILL | NEW SILL

STING WALL

REMOVE EXISTING DOOR AND FRAME

EXISTING WOOD DOOR TO BE REMOVED

EXISTING BRICK VENEER

BRICK TO MATCH EXISTING

EN FLOOR LINE

ENTRANCE TO PARKING EXISTING DOOR OPENING

OURY WALL

LINE OF FINISHED SIDEWALK

ROK EXISTING RADE

EXISTING LEVEL OF MAIN FLOOR

ELEVATION OF WALL AT STREET
SCALE- ¼"= 1'-0"

15 Meeting Street

IRA RAKATANSKY, INC., A.I.A.

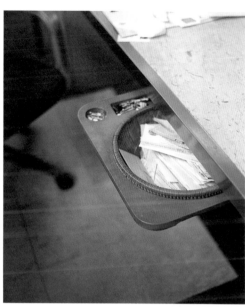

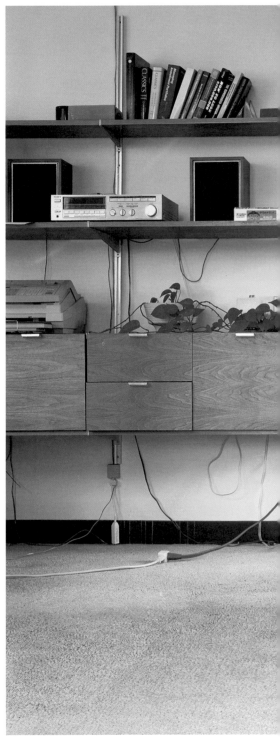

Greenwood Nurseries 1960

Greenwood Nurseries in Warwick,
Rhode Island is still owned and
run by the son of the original client,
Jesse Furtado. Rakatansky met the
Furtados through Ralph Hartman,
the landscape architect for the
Rosen and Blanding homes. The
symmetrical structure consists of
four lattice-covered roofs for partial
shade, three solid roofs for full
shade plants, and four roofs which
house a small garden store. The
functional details, particularly the
trellis and wide-spaced saw-tooth
roofline, create a rhythm that draws
the attentions of passing motorists
on Route 1 near T. F. Green Airport.

Baker House 1960

The Baker House occupies a generous corner lot on Blackstone Boulevard, the only broad tree-filled boulevard on the East Side of Providence, an area consisting of grand 18th and 19th century homes. Mr. Baker had bought a Victorian home, that according to Rakatansky "did not fit these people in any way, shape, or form."

Rakatansky's renovation was radical, removing the second floor and replacing it with a flat roof, which he squared off and extended to form a large overhang on the west side to block the setting sun. By removing fireplaces and servants' staircases, remnants of a pre-modern lifestyle, Rakatansky was able to gain living space despite reducing overall volume.

He reversed the front and rear entrances, placing the new front door on the western side of the house, away from the more trafficked boulevard. He also created a covered entry deck, which extends to the pool house at the other end of the longitudinally proportioned lawn. By transforming a house, which, like its neighbors, had had grandiose historicist façades constructed in the previous century as a monument to the wealth and position of its owners, Rakatansky created a spacious, private house suited to the sentiments of this particular family and their modern lifestyle. Rakatansky considers the Baker house to be, "one of the better things I have done."

The scope of the architectural profession has continuously shrunk and expanded throughout history, assuming greater or lesser authority at different cultural moments and asserting that authority in different ways. Speculation on where that authority is drawn aside, Rakatansky's work maintains all its construction intensity even when focused on such 'low-cultural', profit-driven projects as a bowling alley or a drive-in movie theater. The thoroughness and range of his 1962 drawing set for the Meadow Glen Twin Drive-In in Medford, Massachusetts, says much about the architect's ability to dictate to builder and client; it also says much about the responsibility the architect wittingly assumes by accepting that authority. Designing a drive-in theater sounds like fun. Producing a drawing set for that same program seems to have been a serious task.

In all, the set comprises 20 sheets of drawings. It includes the ticket booths and gate, the concession stand, and the bathrooms. It also defines the abstract geometry, which determines, at the largest scale, the formulation of parking and movie-viewing site lines, and, at the smallest scale, the radii and tangents which form the letters for the drive-in's signage. This range of scale represents a life-long interest: Rakatansky's early design for a reversible dining and lounge chair, his drawings for andirons and the closet hooks in his own house on which he hangs his belt all indicate his ability to operate at the scale of object design. The same minute attention surfaces in the architectural detailing as well, in which both standard and custom solutions are at stake. His abiding investment in the act of efficient, everyday construction as fundamental to the conception of his architecture is evident here, in the way expedient steel I-sections define the zig-zag line of the drive-in's signature entry pavilions or in the way steel, plaster, masonry units and concrete are used for the circular concession stand and projection tower. There are aspects to the set that relate directly to the status of the architectural profession circa 1962.

It may or may not be equitable to compare the drive-in drawing set to the architectural set issued by the office of Eero Saarinen for the CBS Building (1960–65), a mere 26 sheets in which drawings for push plates and telephone booths were given equal attention to the plans which rendered the geometry of the bearing façade on each floor. Of course a skyscraper in midtown New York City for a powerful corporation invested in representing its power is an unlikely comparison to a drive-in theater in small colonial-era town north of Boston. The comparison rests, however, on the seriousness with which every eventuality of construction and fabrication was seen to be within the architect's purview. The density of information in both compact sets implies trust between the architect and his 'first audience'. This is perhaps the darker side of construction transparency: the enormous responsibility on the part of the architect to give appropriate and accurate directives to those whose labor is wholeheartedly and in good faith invested in making architecture.

In the Meadow Glen set, a half-dozen sheets are dedicated to the entry pavilions.

Meadow Glen Twin Drive-In 1962

In the late 1950s and early 1960s Rakatansky was able to secure an increasing number of commercial commissions. In almost every case, these commissions were driven by strong, entrepreneurial individuals who saw architecture as a way to define their public image. His relationship with these individuals extended his architectural philosophy—an enclosure of space around life for a specific site—to the tighter profit margins and fast-paced construction schedule of a business-driven project.

The developers of the Meadow Glen Twin Drive-In were two partners: Julius Riffkin owned the movie licenses and Philip Lowe ran the concessions. The partners arrived

in Rakatansky's office based upon the success of his Shipyard Drive-In built by Melvin Berry. Originally, the Meadow Glen development was also to include a motel with picture windows facing the screen and speakers in each room.

The first drawings date from October of 1961, with the final construction set produced from February through September of 1962, including construction process revisions. The drive-in, with a capacity for more than 500 cars, was operational by the time construction was completed on the Medford segment of I-93 in 1963. It closed in the late 1970s, and was demolished to build a mall in the 1980s.

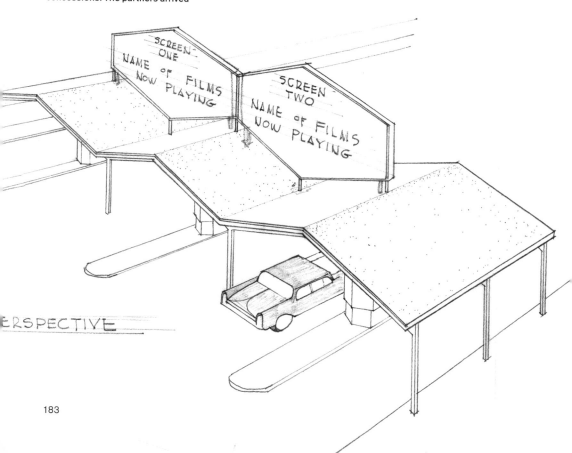

SHEET TWO calls out the designations of all the
steel I-sections used in the primary roof structure,
deeper at the roof peak, lighter at the cricket; it
shows the welded factory-made bents as well as the
on-site bent to column and bent to purlin connections. The structure of the signage is carried separately, by round tube steel columns, which penetrate the roof offset from its peak, to bypass the
purlin. Subtly and effectively, architecture and
signage are differentiated by the I- and round-
column structure. Care has also been taken in the
designation of other details. The 1 x 4 dimensional
lumber, which carries the wood decking between
the steel purlins is kept as thin as possible. The
detail developed to protect the decking and the
1 x 4s from water penetration at the signage column
is equally well-considered: lead-coated copper,
bent to form a custom ring-shape, runs as flashing
beneath the asphalt shingles barely past the depth
of the 1 x 4s, so as not to interfere visually with the
interpenetration of the two structures. Other subtle decisions, such as the side elevation which
shows the end wall slightly lower than the steel
structural beam above it — again, the structure is
legible as independent — and the terse designation
'flush door' in the end wall, witness the fact that
everything has been considered. At the same time,
it is an eminently competent drawing for the contractor who needs to order materials and find
answers on site.

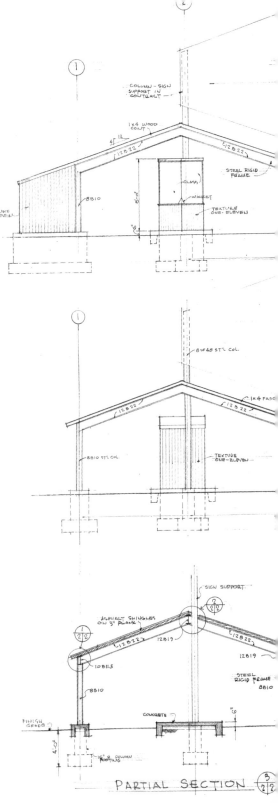

PARTIAL SECTION

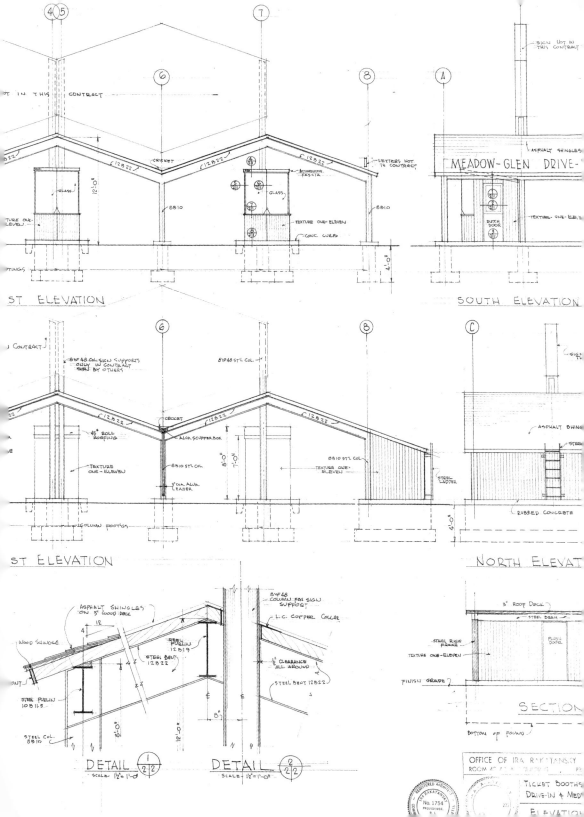

④⑤ ⑦ ⑥ ⑧ Ⓐ

SIGN NOT IN
THIS CONTRACT

OT IN THIS CONTRACT

ASPHALT SHINGLES

MEADOW-GLEN DRIVE-

⑥ 12 B 22 CRICKET 12 B 22 12 B 22

LETTERS NOT
IN CONTRACT

ALUMINUM
FASCIA

GLASS

GLASS

TEXTURE-ONE-ELEN

12'-0"

8 B 10

TEXTURE ONE-
ELEVEN

DUTCH
DOOR

8 B 10

TURE ONE-
ELEVEN

TEXTURE ONE-ELEVEN

CONC. CURB

TINGS

4'-0"

ST ELEVATION

SOUTH ELEVATION

⑥ ⑧ Ⓒ

CONTRACT

8×F 48 COL SIGN SUPPORTS
ONLY IN CONTRACT
SIGN BY OTHERS

8×F 48 ST'L COL.

SIGN
T

12 B 22 CRICKET 12 B 22 C 12 B 22

ASPHALT SHING

45° ROLL
ROOFING

ALUM SCUPPER BOX

STEE

8 B 10 ST'L COL

8 B 10 STL COL.

STEEL
LADDER

TEXTURE
ONE - ELEVEN

TEXTURE ONE-
ELEVEN

8'-0"

7'-0"

5"DIA. ALUM.
LEADER

COLUMN FOOTINGS

RUBBED CONCRETE

4'-0"

ST ELEVATION

NORTH ELEVAT

ASPHALT SHINGLES
ON 3" WOOD DECK

8×F 48
COLUMN FOR SIGN
SUPPORT

3" ROOF DECK

STEEL BEAM

12
4

L.C. COPPER COLLAR

STEEL
PURLIN
12 B 19

STEEL RIGID
FRAME

FLUSH
DOOR

WOOD SHINGLE

STEEL BENT
12 B 22

TEXTURE ONE-ELEVEN

NT

¾" CLEARANCE
ALL AROUND

FINISH GRADE

STEEL PURLIN
10 B 11.5

STEEL BENT 12 B 22

8"

SECTION

STEEL COL.
8 B 10

8'-0"

12'-0"

BOTTOM OF FOUND

DETAIL 1/2/2
SCALE: 1½"=1'-0"

DETAIL 2/2/2
SCALE: 1½"=1'-0"

OFFICE OF IRA RAKATANSKY
ROOM 4

TICKET BOOTHS
DRIVE-IN 4 MED

ELEVATION

REGISTERED ARCHITECT
No. 1754
PROVIDENCE
R.I.

SHEET FOUR, a later page of revisions, offers another example of this insistence on architectural integrity in everyday detailing. In terms of expedient structural integrity, it might have been possible to connect the steel frame roof to the wood-framed ticket booths below it to keep the building from wracking along its vertical dimension. In architectural terms, this would have meant losing the reading of the roof structure as independent. Rakatansky instead chose to use diagonal tension cables, threaded through pre-drilled holes in the steel. To keep the cables at precisely the angle described by the diagonal of the structural bay, the detail specifies 'steel wedges' – custom steel tube used as washers against standard nuts. This logical and direct-seeming solution compounds the difficulty of the detail multiple times: the contractor must find a metal worker to make these pieces, they must arrive at the site in adequate quantity and on time, the geometric tolerances must be accounted for, the predrilled holes must be accurate, and so on. Regardless of all that, the detail is infinitely better suited to sustaining the architectural concept. For a contemporary architect, a design decision such as this one is taken with a sense of dread at its potential pitfalls. For Rakatansky, even in the case of an expediently and inexpensively built project, decisions such as this one were taken many times over, with conviction about the ability of the building trades to execute them and about their clear importance for the architecture, even if not consciously appreciated by the building's audience.

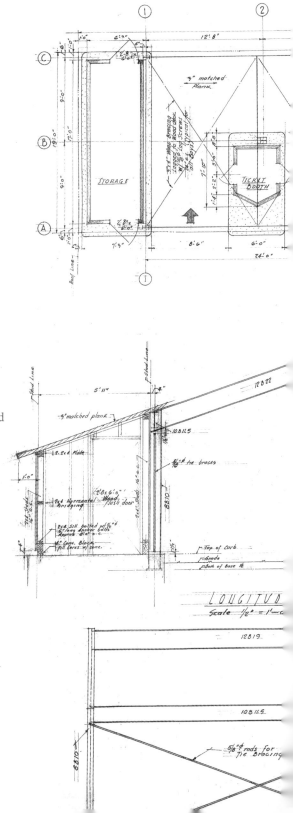

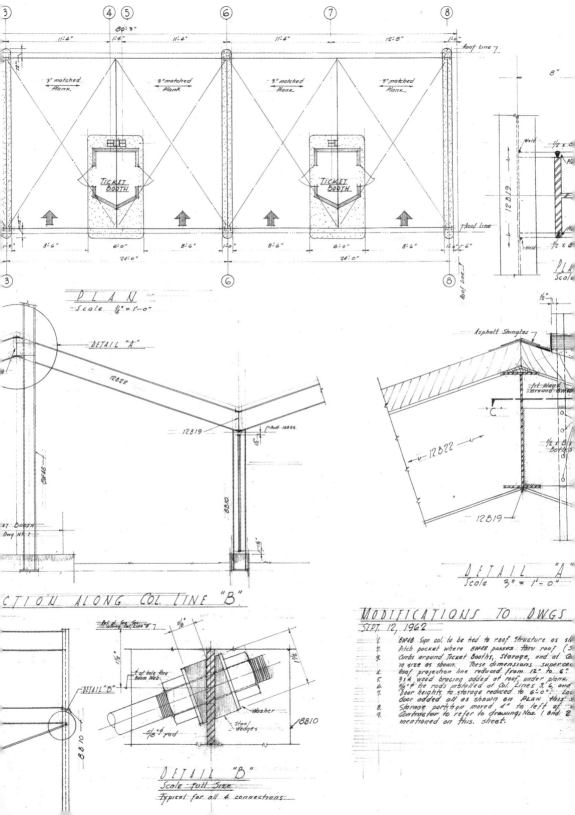

SHEETS THREE AND FIVE are dedicated to the lettering and signage. Each letter, including its precisely scalloped serifs, is drafted at the scale of 1"=1'-0", for use as a template in production. In the lower right corner of sheet 3, the light boxes into which the corrugated plastic letters will be placed are detailed, as if cabinetry. Tapered stops hold the plastic in place; galvanized butt hinges with brass pins are specified so that the light bulbs can be changed. Looking at the precise drawings of such architecturally marginal elements, one wonders why Rakatansky and his client did not simply specify, for example, neon tubes, bent into the letters needed. The fact that they did not might also begin to explain the impulse that resulted in the detailing of the elevator board, push plates and telephone booths in the CBS building as perhaps not only the desire for a corporate Gesamtkunstwerk. 'Specification' did not end with a catalogue page or produce endless construction documents. Saarinen's 26-sheet architectural set sufficed to determine in a binding way both details that were standard and those that were inventions. In the case of the drive-in, the malleability of such 'semi-products' as wood studs, plywood decking, sheet flashing and steel columns – items that arrived on site standardized but indeterminate in their formal character – supported the architect and the construction worker's complicity in shifting the boundary between custom and standard. The comfort with this malleability already evident in Rakatansky's Thief River Falls Library detail page and developed over years of fiddling with standard frame construction translates here into the ability to design *everything*, and to see it realized. It is comparable to what Saarinen and CBS achieved, on the basis of an entirely different set of power relationships.

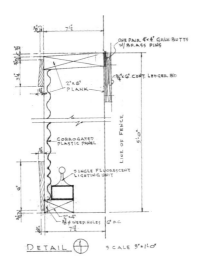

DETAIL SCALE 3"=1'-0"

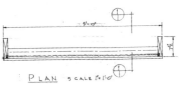

PLAN SCALE 1"=1'-0"

21 SHADOW BOXES REQUIRED FOR SIGN LETTERS

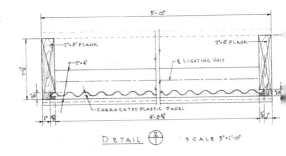

DETAIL ② SCALE 3"=1'-0"

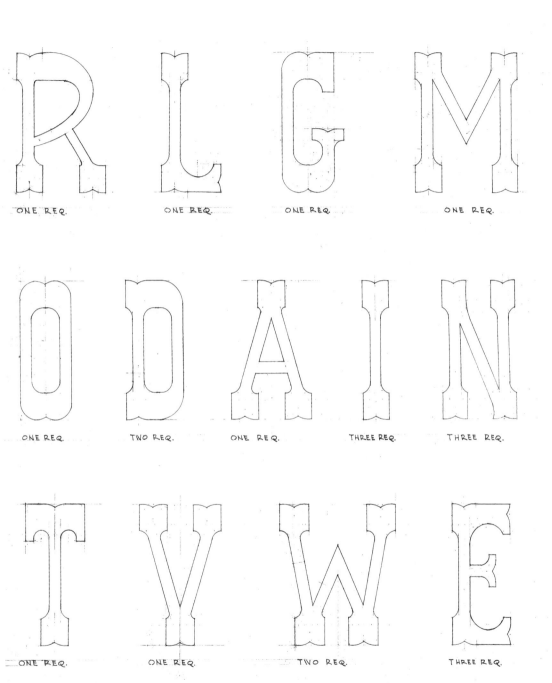

R — ONE REQ. L — ONE REQ. G — ONE REQ. M — ONE REQ.

O — ONE REQ. D — TWO REQ. A — ONE REQ. I — THREE REQ. N — THREE REQ.

T — ONE REQ. V — ONE REQ. W — TWO REQ. E — THREE REQ.

ELEVATIONS OF SIGN LETTERS (ALL LETTERS 42" HIGH)
SCALE 1"=1'-0"

189

Church of God and Saints of Christ 1964

The Church of God and Saints of Christ Tabernacle, constructed on a very tight budget on the south side of Providence addresses the needs of a very unusual congregation. When first approached by the head of the church, Levi Plummer, Rakatansky knew little about the group's religious beliefs, practiced by its 68,000 U.S. members: it is an African-American congregation which worships as Christ did – that is, as Jews.

Rakatansky did not find a faith based project incompatible with his secular views, believing the space he created for the Church of God and Saints of Christ to be sacred. If not, he would have considered it, in his own words, 'ungodly'.

As the church was located in a neighborhood prone to break-ins and vandalism, it was conceived as a 'fortress' from the outside. There are few windows to the exterior. Instead, an interior patio brings light into the center of the building and organizes the spaces. A tree, short shrubs and a monument inhabit the enclosed patio, which also helps to circulate air in lieu of air conditioning. The building's central artery allows for views to the offices and classrooms, as well as to an open stairwell leading up to the social hall.

The Providence Church of God and Saints of Christ continues to worship in the space, and it remains a powerful example of Rakatansky's conception of sacral Modern space as developed during his career for different faiths and practices. It reflects the autobiographical and cultural themes, which he first architecturalized in his thesis project of 1945.

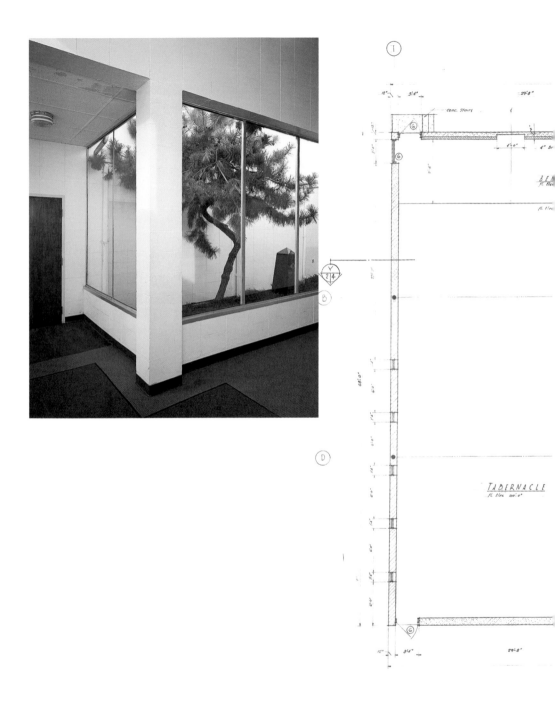

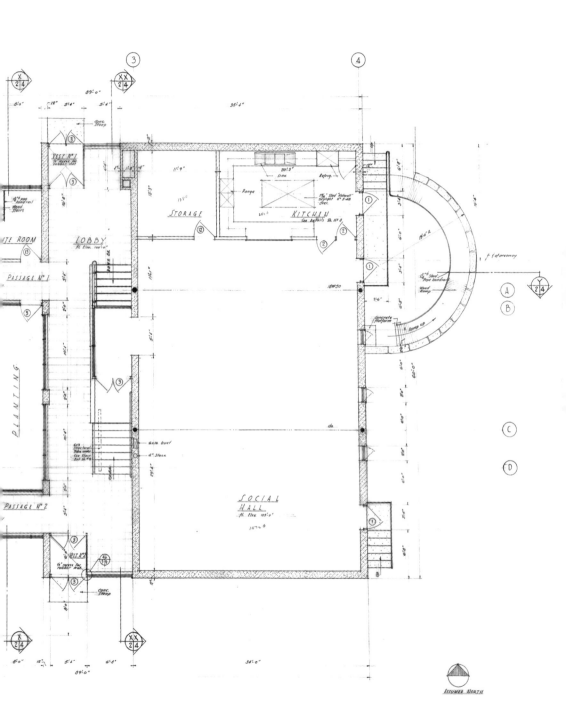

ASSUMED NORTH

The
Face
of
Religion

TEXT BY ROBERT D. WHITAKER

JOURNAL-BULLETIN PHOTOS BY H. RAYMOND BALL

Landscaping is held up by reconstruction of Cranston Street. Douglas Construction and Supply Corp., Providence, was the contractor.

Church Plans Welfare Program at New Site

Its new tabernacle dedicated last Sunday, the Church of God and Saints of Christ is looking forward to completion of its furnishings and landscaping and the possible opening of a social service agency under the federal antipoverty program.

The new sanctuary with its synagogue-like appointments is on the street level. Still lacking pews, it will seat 200 to 250 on folding chairs.

A lower level in an adjoining portion of the building contains the church offices, lavatories and three classrooms. The level above these is occupied by a multi-purpose room for meetings and dinners and the kitchen.

The proposed social service agency, is indirectly designed to deal more "on level" with persons whose personal and social problems "are deeply

It will serve persons whose problems "are deeply rooted, whose despair and deprivation seem unsolvable by present, existing agencies in the community.

"Such individuals need the skills of professional personnel who can relate to them in simple, understandable terms," according to the statement.

The proposed budget for this program is $40,000 a year for a fully operating agency and the church is seeking antipoverty funds for its operation.

Miss Beatrice K. Phillips, now working in the Child Development Study conducted by Brown University, is the proposed director for the agency.

The First Tabernacle, as the new building is called, is between Cranston and Lester Streets across Dodge Street from the new Catholic Student Center which was dedicated on May 21.

It is the sixth home of the Providence congregation which was incorporated in 1906 by the Rev. Allan Warren,

The church has previously worshiped in quarters on Winter Street, at 422 Washington St. and 10 Cranston St.; purchased the former Pond Street Baptist Church building in 1948 and later moved into the quarters of a former Spiritualist church at 32 Haskins St. when the Pond Street structure was razed for Route 95.

A black-topped church parking lot will be expanded to provide offstreet space for about 50 cars when the Providence Redevelopment Agency completes a transaction involving the abandonment of Lester Street.

Under this transaction, the Church of God and Saints of Christ expects to acquire title to the center of Lester Street. The Ebenezer Baptist Church at 80 Dodge St., expects to acquire the other half of Lester Street.

Landscaping will be completed after the finishing of the widening of Cranston Street, according to Ira Rakatansky, architect for the church.

The Church of God and

railway cook, in Lawrence, Kans. International headquarters are now in Belleville, Va.

Its doctrines include a belief that the Negroes are descendants of the "lost tribes of Israel" and its religion is described as a Judaism and the religion of Jesus.

The church's Sabbath starts at sundown on Friday and ends at sundown on Saturday.

The church observes the Jewish Day of Atonement and the Passover — "all Jewish holidays except those that are post-Biblical, as political expediency," according to the prepared statement.

The church uses both the Old and New Testaments and practices Communion and baptism, the latter by immersion outdoors in running waters.

The church uses no musical instruments and the Providence unit has a highly trained a cappella choir.

Among furnishings still to be acquired are pews for the sanctuary and a Torah scroll

Pastor's eye view of sanctuary, from behind the bema.

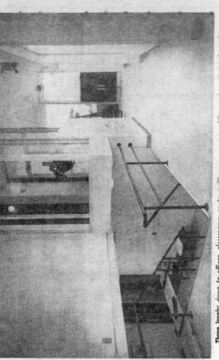

One of the classrooms

Three levels: down to offices, classrooms; up to multi-purpose room, while sanctuary is to the right.

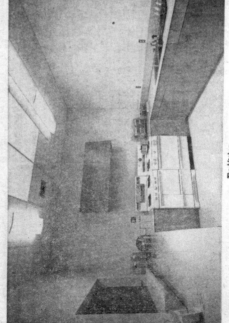

The kitchen

1919
*Born to Benjamin and Martha
(Bornstein) Rakatansky*

1942
*Diploma in Architecture, Rhode Island
School of Design*

1944
*Works for one year in the office of
Marcel Breuer on these projects: Almy,
Bigelow & Washurn Department
Store; War Memorial; Pencil Points/
Pittsburgh Plate Glass Company House
Competition; Geller House*

Thief River Falls Library Addition,
Harvard University (Marcel Breuer,
instructor)

Apartment Building, Harvard
University (Breuer, instructor)

Redevelopment of South End,
Boston, Harvard University (Walter
Gropius and Breuer, instructors)

1

Chronology
1919–

1945

B. Arch, Harvard University [1]

Awarded Wheelwright Fellowship, Harvard University

Reform Temple, thesis project, Harvard University

"Synagogue for Providence, R. I.: A thesis designed by Ira Rakatansky, Harvard University," *Progressive Architecture*, December: 66–67.

1946

M. Arch, Harvard University

Establishes independent design practice within the office of architect Samuel Morino

Furniture for office of Dr. Fish, Providence

Hill House, Rehoboth, Mass. *unbuilt*

Kenner House, Seekonk, Mass. *unbuilt*

1947

Braude Study-Library, Providence

Genser House, Providence *unbuilt*

Halsband House, East Greenwich, R.I.

1948

Establishes collaborative practice with engineer Samuel Lerner

Medical Office Building, Providence

Miller House, Providence

Weinstein House, Providence

Agnew, Dorothy. "New Role for the Carriage House: Stable Transformed Into 6 Rooms of Glamour" [Miller House], *Providence Sunday Journal*, August 1, Home Building, Real Estate Section: V-1, 5.

Agnew, Dorothy. "As Modern as Tomorrow: Old East Greenwich Is Setting for New House with Latest Design Features" [Halsband House], *Providence Sunday Journal*, October 31, Home, Real Estate Section: V-1.

"East Side Sees New Design in Bricks" [Medical Office Building], *Providence Evening Bulletin*.

"Architect Blasts Brown's New Moat," *Brown Daily Herald*, December 7: 1.

1949

Establishes own architectural practice in the Arcade Building, Providence

Camp Walt Whitman Dining Hall, Pike, N.H.

Reversible Chair

Weisberg House, Newport

Agnew, Dorothy. "Room for Father" [Braude Study-Library], *Providence Sunday Journal*, December 4, Building, Real Estate Section: V-1, 3.

1950s

2

1950
Horn House, Rehoboth, Mass.

Wax House, Providence

Feingold House, Providence [2]

Zitserman House, Providence

"House, East Greenwich, Rhode Island: Ira Rakatansky, Designer" [Halsband House], *Progressive Architecture*, October: 79–81.

1951
Blanding House, Greene, R.I.

Agnew, Dorothy. "Pint-Size Modern: Daringly-Different House Blends Cinder Blocks, Glass, Wood" [Wax House], *Providence Sunday Journal*, August 12, Home Section: V-1, 5.

Agnew, Dorothy. "High Style in Newport: Modern Home Sits on Hillside in City of Quaint Dwellings" [Weisberg House], *Providence Sunday Journal*, August 25, Home Section: V-1.

1952
Marries Lenore (Gray)

Bernstein House, North Swansea, Mass. *unbuilt*

Osburne House, Hampton, Conn.

Reversible Chair receives U.S. Patent No. 2,602,491 on July 8

Agnew, Dorothy. "A House That Hides Its Charms: Remodeling Job Saves Face of Modest Cottage in Greene" [Blanding House], *Providence Sunday Journal*, January 20, Home Section: V-1.

1953
Birth of daughter Lynn

Blanding's Pharmacy, Providence

Pollock House, Attleboro, Mass.

"More space within old walls" [Blanding House], *Better Homes and Gardens*, September: 199–200.

1954
Designs own house in Lincoln

Falk House, Narragansett, R.I.

Rakatansky House, Lincoln, R.I.

Spring Green Memorial Church, Warwick, R.I.

Agnew, Dorothy. "A Place for the Magazines" *Providence Sunday Journal*, February 28, Home: V-1.

Agnew, Dorothy. "Designed for a Wooded Hill" [Pollock House], *Providence Sunday Journal*, October 31, Home Section: V-1, 10.

[Spring Green Memorial Church], *Providence Evening Bulletin*, August 27.

1955
Dunn House, Lexington, Mass. [3]

Franek House, East Greenwich, R.I.

Rosen House, Pawtucket, R.I.

Starr House, Lexington, Mass. [4]

Ziskind House, Middletown, R.I.

Hahn, Donna Nicolas. "Dare to be Different" [Weisberg House], *Perfect Home*, February: 12–13.

[Spring Green Memorial Church], *Rhode Island Baptist*, May: cover and 3.

[Rakatansky House, Lincoln], *Moebel-Decoration*: 203–205.

1956
Miller House, Providence

Agnew, Dorothy. "An Architect Designs His Own Dream House" [Rakatansky House, Lincoln], *Providence Sunday Journal*, January 29, Home Section: V-1.

Agnew, Dorothy. "A Summer Home in Middletown" [Ziskind House], *Providence Sunday Journal*, July 22, Home Section: V-1.

"If you will it, it is not a dream"

TEMPLE BETH AM — WARWICK, RHODE ISLAND — 1958

1958
Designs own house in Providence

Blieden House, Warwick, R.I.

Levin House, Woonsocket, R.I.

Myers House and Office, Providence

Rakatansky House, Providence

Temple Beth Am, Warwick, R.I. [6]

Ten Pin Lanes Bowling, Providence [7]

Agnew, Dorothy. "Spacious Home Utilizes Small Lot" [Rosen House], *Providence Sunday Journal*, May 4, Home Section: H-1.

Agnew, Dorothy. "Modern Widow's Walk" [Rogers House], *Providence Sunday Journal*, August 31, Home Section: H-1.

"Planned Jewish Temple in Warwick" [Temple Beth-Am], *Providence Sunday Journal*, September 14, Metropolitan Section: M-1.

1959
Moves office to Meeting Street

15 Meeting Street, Providence

Agnew, Dorothy. "Architect Designs Home For Himself" [Rakatansky House, Providence], *Providence Sunday Journal*, March 22, Home Section: H-1.

Agnew, Dorothy. "Warwick Home Faces Secluded Garden" [Blieden House], *Providence Sunday Journal*," June 7, Home Section: H-1.

Thompson, Jack. "Bowling in R.I. Becomes Organized Giant of Sports" [Ten Pin Lanes Bowling], *Providence Sunday Journal*, December 20: N-52.

1957
Birth of son Mark

Rogers House, Weekapaug, R.I.

Rogge House, Stamford, Conn.

Shipyard Drive-In, Providence

Von Storch House, North Kingston, R.I. *unbuilt* [5]

Agnew, Dorothy. "Neighbors Look Twice" [Franek House], *Providence Sunday Journal*, January 13, Home Section: V-1.

"Drive-In Theatres: A 'Sunken' Playground for Safety" [Shipyard Drive-In], *Boxoffice*, 5 October: 32–35 [Modern Theatre section].

Agnew, Dorothy. "Compact Luxury: Barn Goes Modern" [Miller House], *Providence Sunday Journal*, October 27, Home Section: V-1.

1960s

10

1960
Atlantic Bowling, East Providence

Baker House, Providence

Greenwood Nurseries, Warwick, R.I.

Simon House, Providence [8]

1961
Reck House, Acapesket, Mass.

1962
Meadow-Glen Twin Drive-In,
Medford, Mass.

Burnight House, Barrington, R.I. [9]

Hanson, Edward C. "Remolded
Carriage House Has Silo Bath"
[Burnight House], *Providence Sunday
Journal*, March 4, Home Section: H-1.

1963
Waring House, Virgin Islands

Corey, Madeliene. "Traditional vs.
Contemporary," *Providence Sunday
Journal*, March 10, Women's Section:
W-1.

1964
Church of God and Saints of Christ,
Providence

40 Westminster Office Building,
Providence *unbuilt* [10]

8

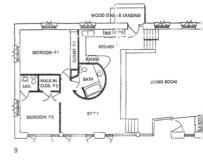

9

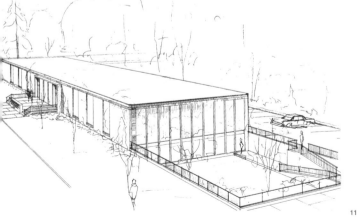

1965

Whitaker, Robert D. "Church Plans Welfare Program at New Site" [Church of God and Saints of Christ], *Providence Journal*, July 10: 3.

1966

"First Hartford Realty to Build 22-Story Building in Providence" [40 Westminster], *Hartford Courant*, May 29, Sunday Edition: 2D.

"Providence to Get 22-Story Building" [40 Westminster], *New York Times*, June 26, Sunday Real Estate Section: R12.

1967

Gardner House, Pascoag, R.I.
unbuilt

Teamster Administration Building, Providence [11]

1968

Chisholm House, Barrington, R.I.

Gravdahl House, Jamestown, R.I.

Harper House, Little Compton, R.I. [12]

1969

Aber House, Tiverton, R.I.

General Wine Company Warehouse, Providence

Hanson, Edward C. "Ledge-hugging bayside house has a feeling of all outdoors" [Gravdahl House], *Providence Sunday Journal*, November 16, Homes Section: H-1.

1970s – 1980s

15

1970
Collier House, Little Compton, R.I.

1971
Bishop Plummer (Senior) House,
Suffolk, Va.

Connecticut Laborers' Union,
Hartford, Conn.

Patterson House, Jamestown, R.I. [13]

1972
Connecticut Laborers' Union, West
Haven, Conn.

1973
Ward, John. "The Pattersons cut into
hill for new Jamestown view" [Patterson
House], *Providence Sunday Journal*,
October 14, Accent on the Arts, Homes
Section: F-1.

1974
Gifford House, Matunuck, R.I.

1975
Peterborough Convalescence
Homes, Peterborough, N.H.

1976
Persimmon Restaurant, Providence

13

14

16

1977
Mayflower Savings and Loan Office Building, Providence *unbuilt* [14]

1978
Arnold House, Tiverton, R.I. [15]

1979
Brown University Faculty Club addition, Providence

1980
Church of God and Saints of Christ, Suffolk, Va.

Starr-Naylor House, Brookline, Mass.

Chiappinelli, Robert. "You don't have to be Jewish ..." [Church of God and Saints of Christ], *Providence Evening Bulletin*, November 17: A-3.

1981
Rakatansky Office Addition, Providence

1982
Bishop Plummer, Jr. House, Suffolk, Va.

Sprague House, Barrington, R.I.

1983
Saber House, Barrington, R.I. [16]

1984
New England Laborers' Training Academy (Dining Hall), Pomfret, Conn.

1985
Church of God and Saints of Christ (sanctuary addition), Suffolk, Va.

New England Laborers' Training Academy (dormitory), Pomfret, Conn.

1986
Holocaust Memorial, Providence

Slepkow House, Providence

1988
New England Laborers' Training Academy, Hopkinton, Mass.

1990s—

1992
Rosen House, Pawcatuck, Conn.

2002
Anthony Alofsin. *The Struggle for Modernism: Architecture, Landscape Architecture, and City Planning at Harvard* (New York: Norton, 2002), pp 190, 211.

2003
Gunther-Rosenberg, Avis. "House of the Week: Providence contemporary stands out from the crowd" [Weinstein House], *Providence Journal Bulletin*, 11 October, Real Estate Section: E-04.

2005
Exhibit of early drawings titled "Ira Rakatansky: Providence Modern Houses from 1947–1978" held at the RISD Architecture Department

Rakatansky in 2006 in the home he
completed nearly 50 years earlier

Illustration Credits

Photographers

A) Laurence E. Tilley
B) H. Raymond Ball, ©*Providence Journal*
C) Thomas D. Stevens, ©*Providence Journal*
D) Ezra Stoller, ©Esto Photographics
E) Richard Garrison
F) Harold E. Winslow, ©*Providence Journal*
G) Thad Russell
H) John Caserta
I) Harry A. Scheer, ©*Providence Journal*
J) Mark Rakatansky
K) Kimberly Holcombe

Drawings/Publications/Other

L) ©*Providence Journal* and *Providence Sunday Journal*
M) ©Harvard University GSD Archive, Loeb Library
N) Ira Rakatansky / Office of Ira Rakatansky, AIA
O) *Progressive Architecture*
P) Arber-French & Co. Photographers
Q) Property of current resident

Pages with multiple credits list sources from top to bottom. Every reasonable attempt has been made to identify owners of copyright.

Credit by page

–	--	--	91 A	121 H	---	181 H
2 A	--	62 N	92 C	122 P	152 G	---
–	--	63 N	93 N	123 P	153 G	183 N N
4 C	34 N	64 N	94 C	124 G	154 G	---
–	--	65 N	95 C	125 G G	155 G G	185 N
–	37 N	66 N	96 C	126 N	156 N N	---
8 L	--	67 B	97 C	---	157 H	187 N
–	39 M	68 L	98 N	128 P	158 H	188 N
10 L	--	--	--	---	---	189 N
--	41 M	70 G G	100 L	130 G	160 H	190 Q H
--	42 N	71 N	---	131 G	161 H	191 H
13 L	--	72 H	102 G G	132 C	162 H	192 H
--	--	73 H	103 G	---	163 H	193 N
15 L	45 N	74 L	104 G	134 P	164 H	194 L
16 C	46 O	--	105 G	135 C	165 H	---
--	47 N N	76 E	106 G	136 N	166 H	196 N
--	48 N	77 E	---	---	167 H	---
19 M N M	--	78 I	108 G	138 N	168 H	198 N N N
--	50 E	--	109 G	---	169 H	199 N N N
21 D N	51 E	80 N	110 L	140 L	170 H	200 N J L
--	52 O	--	---	---	---	201 N J J N
--	53 G G	82 N N	112 C C	142 G	172 Q	202 G K
--	54 G G	83 N	113 N	143 B N	---	203 N N
--	55 E	--	114 N	144 G	174 H H H H	---
--	56 F	85 B	---	145 G	175 H	205 H
--	--	86 B	116 N	146 G	176 H	---
--	58 G	--	---	147 G	177 H	---
--	59 F	88 L	118 L	148 B	178 H	---
--	--	--	---	149 G	---	
--	--	90 A	120 H	150 G	180 H	

Book Credits

Editors John Caserta and Lynnette Widder

Essays Joan Ockman and Lynnette Widder

Design John Caserta

Project texts Erin Eckhold

Chronology Mark Rakatansky

Research assistants Bryan Bieser, David Knouf,
  Kyle Marshall, Damir Vukovljak

Document photography Erik Gould

Production assistants Lindsay Kinkade, Elise Porter

Film processing Renaissance Creative Imaging

Image archiving and proofing The Design Office

Acknowledgments

This book was made possible by a grant from the Graham
Foundation for Advanced Studies in the Fine Arts and
by funding through the Velux Corporation and the RISD
Professional Development Fund.

We would like to acknowledge and thank the following
individuals and organizations for their support:
Dawn Barrett, Denise Bastien, Laurie Whitehill Chong,
Mary Daniels, Nick DePace, Julie Fry, Pamela Harrington,
Margaret Lewis, Jeremy Mickel, Jaime Marland, Steven
McDonald, Frank Mullin, Mark Rakatansky, Mark Rapp,
William Stout, *The Providence Journal* and their photography
department from 1946 to 1964, Esto Photographics,
BOXOFFICE Media, and the Loeb Library at Harvard
University.

Contemporary photographs would not have been possible
without the hospitality and generosity of the current
residents. We thank you for your time and interest.

A special thank you to Ira Rakatansky and Lenore Gray.
You have opened your doors to us countless times and have
aided us in opening others.

Skylights

JOHN CASERTA is an information designer, critic in graphic design at Rhode Island School of Design and founder of The Design Office. He received an MFA in graphic design from the Yale School of Art and a BA in journalism from the University of North Carolina. In 2004 he was the Fulbright Fellow in the Arts to Italy, where he curated available artifacts, photographed buildings and landscapes, and interviewed towns-people in a small southern Italian village. In 2007 John founded The Design Office, an organization that supports independent designers by providing workspace, equipment, community, and by initiating individual and collaborative projects and products.

LYNNETTE WIDDER's career has included work as a practicing architect in the U.S., Germany and German-speaking Switzerland; she is currently partner in the New York-based firm aardvarchitecture. From 1994 to 1996, she was English language editor of the Berlin-based German-English quarterly *Daidalos*. She has completed scholarly research in the area of post-war German architecture and nineteenth-century German architectural theory, and extensive German-to-English translations of architectural and art historical texts and books. For the past fifteen years she has taught design, construction and history/theory of architecture at the ETH Zurich, the University of British Columbia, Cornell University, Columbia University and the Rhode Island School of Design, where she is Associate Professor and Department Head. She holds degrees from Barnard College and Columbia University, and is working on a dissertation in architectural history at the University of Zürich.